The 80th Division in World War I

The Battle for Bois d'Ogons, Oct. 4-6, 1918.

Gary Schreckengost

80thdivision.com

Amazon.com

To Our Departed Comrades
And Their Families.
The 80th Division Only Moves Forward!

Copyright © 2016 Gary Schreckengost
All rights reserved.
All photographs either belong to the 80th Division Veterans' Association or the U.S. Army Signal Corps.
Frontispiece: "Sunday Morning at Cunel."

80th Division Association
www.80thdivision.com
Amazon.com

CONTENTS

Preface, 4.

Chapters

1. Before the Battle of Bois d'Ogons, 84.

2. The Hell of Bois d'Ogons and *KRIEMHILDE* (October 4-6), 117.

3. The Battle for Ferme Madeleine (Oct. 7-31, 1918), 153.

Bibliography, 213.

About the Author, 215.

Preface

America's 80th "Blue Ridge" Infantry Division was constituted on August 5, 1917, as part of the National Army (today's Army Reserve), with headquarters at Camp Lee, Virginia. The division itself consisted primarily of drafted men or "Selectees" from Virginia, West Virginia, and Pennsylvania and adopted the now-famous moniker "Blue Ridge Division," as the wondrous Blue Ridge Mountains of the Appalachian chain connected all three states and its peoples. When thrown into combat during the bone-crushing and war-ending Meuse-Argonne Offensive of September-November 1918, the 80th Division was also *the only American division to breach all four of the vaunted German Hindenburg defensive lines during the Meuse-Argonne Offensive* (*HAGEN, GISELHER, KRIEMHILDE,* and *FREYA*). In fact, the place where it breached *KRIEMHILDE*, the strongest of the lines, there now sits America's largest Soldier cemetery in France, standing as stoic reminder of the 80th Division's desperate and heroic actions. Because of its operations and the operations of many other American divisions, the Associated Powers (the Allies plus the United States) were finally able to smash the near-impregnable German defenses and push north to the outskirts of Sedan, ultimately ending the war with a German defeat. All told, the 80th "Blue Ridge" Division advanced some twenty miles across the most-heavily defended place on the earth at the time, suffered over 6,000 casualties—over half of its infantry strength—and killed or captured thousands of German soldiers in order to achieve ultimate victory. Their actions so inspired their Regular Army division commander, Maj. Gen. Adelbert Cronkhite to loudly proclaim: "The 80th Division Always Moves Forward!"

One of the missions of the 80th Division Association is to try to help Blue Ridge Division Soldiers, family members, and interested parties better understand "what it was like" for its Soldiers in the service of America's Blue Ridge Division.

This book is an effort to fill that need.

As such, *this is the historically accurate story* of a representative Dough Boy who served with America's Blue Ridge Division during World War I: Automatic Rifleman Joe Riddle of Company B, 1st Battalion, 318th Infantry Regiment, 159th Infantry Brigade. In Volume 1, read how and why Joe joined the Army in 1917, what training was like at Camp Lee, Virginia, how he was shipped to France, what it was like serving with the British in Artois and

Picardy, France, and what the division did during the American First Army's first offensie of the war: the Saint Mihiel Offensive.

This book is actually part of a series. The heart of the series revolves around Volumes One and Two. Volume One deals with the assemblage and the training of the division at Camp Lee, Virginia, its service with the British in the Somme, and its participation in the Saint-Mihiel Campaign of 1918. Volume Two is about the division's heavy combat in the Meuse-Argonne Offensive, its aftermath, and coming home. This volume is a truncated version of Volume Two.

I'd like to acknowledge the people who helped me complete this project. First, I'd also like to acknowledge my 80th Division Association brothers and sisters who helped me with the research, gathering of pictures, and who said "do it Schreck," in no particular order: Capt. Lee Anthony (U.S.N., ret.), the 80th Division Association's "World War I Historian" and editor of Sergeant Stultz's tome about the division's history during the Great War for Civilization, Maj. Gen. John P. McLaren (U.S.A., ret.), commander emeritus of the 80th Division Association and my commanding officer in Iraq, Mr. Ben Jarratt of the Association who meticulously proofed my manuscript and helped improve it, Mr. Andy Adkins, the Association's "World War II Historian" and author of *You Can't Get Much Closer Than This: Combat with the 80th "Blue Ridge" Division in World War II Europe*, Maj. Dean Dominique (U.S.A., ret.), the author of *One Hell of a War: Patton's 317th Infantry Regiment in WWII*, and Mr. Jeff Wignall, the 2015 National Commander of the Association and author of *Farebersviller 1944*.[1]

Maj. Gary Schreckengost (U.S.A., ret.), 80th Division Association
Cold War, Homeland, Bosnia, and Iraq

---

[1] www.80thdivision.com. The Association consists not only of veterans of the division, but also family members of those who served in the division. Lee Anthony's and Ben Jarratt's ancestors, for example, served in the division during World War I.

1-2

HEADQUARTERS EIGHTIETH DIVISION.

AMERICAN EXPEDITIONARY FORCES.

France, 11 November, 1918.

GENERAL ORDER No. 19.

To the Members of the 80th Division:

The 80th Division Only Moves FORWARD.

It not only moves forward against the enemy, but it moves forward in the estimation of all who are capable of judging its courage, its fighting, and its manly qualities.

In the operations for the period of November 1-5, the division moved forward fifteen and five-eighths miles in an air line.

It always led.

It captured two Huns for every man wounded.

It captured one machine gun for every man wounded.

It captured one cannon for every ten men wounded, besides large quantities of munitions and other stores.

It accomplished these results of vast importance to the success of the general operation, with a far smaller percentage of casualties than in any other division engaged.

It has learned from hard training and experience.

The appreciation of the corps and the Army commanders is expressed in the following:

Telegram from the Commanding General, First Army (dated Nov. 1):

> "The Army Commander desires that you inform the Commander of the 80th Division of the Army Commander's appreciation of his excellent work during the battle of to-day. He desires that you have this information sent to all organizations of that Division as far as may be practicable this night. He fully realizes the striking blow your division has delivered to the enemy this date."

Telegram from the Commanding General, First Army Corps (dated Nov. 1):

> "The corps commander is particularly pleased with the persistent, intelligent work accomplished by your division today which has borne the brunt of the burden."

Letter from the Commanding General, First Army Corps, A.E.F. (dated Nov. 11):

> The corps commander desires that you be informed and that those under your command be informed that in addition to other well deserved commendations received from the Army commander and corps commander, he wishes to express his particular gratification and appreciation of the work of your division from the time it has entered under his command."

It is necessarily a great honor to be allowed to command an organization which earns such commendation.

It is likewise a great honor to belong to such an organization.

I do not know what the future has in store for us.

If it be war, we must and shall sustain our honor and our reputation by giving our best to complete the salvation of our country.

If it be peace, we must and shall maintain our reputation and the honor of our division and the Army, as soldiers of the greatest country on earth, and as right-minded, self-respecting men.

The 80th Division Only Moves FORWARD.

CRONKHITE, Major-General.

1-2

France, 18 March, 1919.

GENERAL ORDERS NO. 12.

The 80th Division, having been instructed to prepare for return to the United States, will pass from the command of this Army Corps on 20 March, 1919.

The 80th Division arrived in France about June 5, 1918. This Division trained with the British Troops and was on active duty with them in the Artois Sector near Arras in July. The Division was in reserve at the battle of ST. MIHIEL, except the 320th Infantry and 315th Machine Gun Battalion, which took part in the operations of the II French Colonial Corps. From September 26 to 29, inclusive, the Division attacked at BETHINCOURT with the III American Corps and advanced nine kilometers in two days. The Division was withdrawn from the line for five days and again attacked on October 4 at NANTILLOIS. In 9 days of heavy fighting through the BOIS DE OGONS an advance of four kilometers was made. The Division was withdrawn from the line October 12 for re-equipment and replacements. The Division moved forward on October 29 and 30 and re-entered the line at ST. JUVIN.

The 80th Division passed under the orders of the I Corps on October 23. On November 1, the Division attacked as the right division of the I Corps and in six days advanced a depth of 24 kilometers. The Division was relieved from the line on November 6, with its patrols on the west bank of the Meuse. From 18 November to 1 December, the Division marched 221 kilometers to the 15th Training Area at Auey-le-Franc. The artillery of the Division was part of the time detached from the Division and was in action at all times from September 26-November 11.

2-2

The Division has remained in the 15th Training Area until its present order to prepare from embarkation to the United States.

The 80th Division was given the difficult tasks on the front line and in accomplishing them made a splendid record. The corps commander desired particularly to express his appreciation for the soldierly achievements of this division during the time it served with the I Army Corps. After returning to the training area where living conditions were not easy and often difficult the spirit of the division has been excellent and has been manifest at all times. The division leaves on the first part of its journey with the corps commander's congratulations for its excellent record and his wishes for a speedy return to the United States and a successful future.

By command of Major-General Wright.

W.M. FASSETT.

Chief of Staff.

OFFICIAL.

Lt.-Col. A.G.D. Adjutant.

HEADQUARTERS EIGHTIETH DIVISION.

AMERICAN EXPEDITIONARY FORCE.

France, 14 May, 1919.

BULLETIN # 113.

The following letter has been received from Lieut. Gen. Robert Lee Bullard, U.S.A., in command of the III Corps, A.E.F., during the Meuse-Argonne Offensive:

"Under the pressure of great events I, at that time commanding the III Corps to which the 80th Division then belonged, failed to cite the gallant conduct of the division in making three successive assaults with great bravery and finally taking and driving the enemy from Bois Ogons in the great battle of the Meuse-Argonne. I cite it now. It was truly admirable. We see it now more plainly in the light of the results that followed. I ask that this be communicated to your gallant division."

The 80th Division was the only A.E.F. division which went into line in the Meuse-Argonne Offensive three times.

By command of Major General Cronkhite:

W.H. Waldron,

Col., General Staff,

Chief of Staff

The 80th Division officially participated in four campaigns during World War I ("The Great War for Civilization") and suffered 6,101 casualties (217 K.I.A. and 5,884 W.I.A.) out of around 28,000 assigned (22% casualty rate, 2% K.I.A., 20% W.I.A.). We were present at the Saint-Mihiel campaign, too, but the Army didn't officially recognize it as a division battle, as only one regiment, the 320th Infantry, was sent into it. The infantry battalions, of course, suffered far greater casualties. The 3/320th Infantry, for example, suffered 600 casualties out of 840 men (71%), which breaks down to 91 K.I.A. (11%) and 509 W.I.A. (60%). By operation, the casualty figures are as follows:

1918 Somme Offensive: 427 casualties (7 K.I.A., 420 W.I.A.).

1918 Meuse-Argonne (Phase I): 1,064 casualties (27 K.I.A., 1,037 W.I.A.) .

1918 Meuse-Argonne (Phase II): 3,551 casualties (1,154 K.I.A., 2,397 W.I.A.).

1918 Meuse-Argonne (Phase III): 1,059 casualties (44 K.I.A., 1,015 W.I.A.).

As for decorations, citations, and awards, the 80th Division received a total of 619, as follows:

Distinguished Service Crosses: 59

Distinguished Service Medals: 20

General Headquarters, A.E.F. Citation: 41

War Dept. Citations: 31

Division Citations: 35

Brigade Citations: 345

Meritorious Service Certificates: 34

Maj. Gen. Adelbert Cronkhite, our beloved division commander. He was the Regular Army coast artillery officer in charge of the Panama Canal Zone before the war.

Cronkhite's primary staff. Col. William Waldron, the division chief of staff, is top center.

Brig. Gen. Charles S. Farnsworth, 159th Inf. Brig. commander and his principal staff (317th and 318th Inf.). He was later promoted to command the 37th "Buckeye Division" in France.

Col. George H. Jamerson, 317th Inf. commander and his principal staff. Most of the 317th Regiment came from western Virginia.

Col. Briant H. Wells, 318th Inf. commander and his principal staff. Most of the 318th came from eastern Virginia.

Brig. Gen. Lloyd M. Brett, 160th Inf. Brig. commander (319th and 320th Inf.). Arguably the best brigadier in the entire A.E.F. Medal of Honor recipient for actions during the Geronimo Campaign, cited for gallantry during the War with Spain, the Philippines, and the Punitive Expedition under Pershing, Superintendent of Yellowstone Nat'l Park, commander of the 4th Cav. Reg't. when war was declared.

Col. Frank S. Cocheu, 319th Inf. commander and his principal staff. Most of the 319th Regt. came from Pittsburgh. Maj. Montague's 3/319th was the most engaged and most successful battalion of the division.

Col. Ora E. Hunt, 320th Infantry Commander and Staff. Most of the 320th Inf. came from the counties surrounding Pittsburgh.

Brig. Gen. Gordon G. Heiner, Commander of the 155th Arty. Brig. and his principal staff. Units from our artillery brigade spent more days in combat than any other of the Blue Ridge Division.

Col. Charles D. Herron and 313th Arty. Staff.

Col. Robert S. Welsh and 314th Arty. Staff. Welsh will eventually command the 155th Arty. Brig.

Col. Russell P. Reeder and 315th Arty. Staff. This was the division's "heavy" artillery regiment.

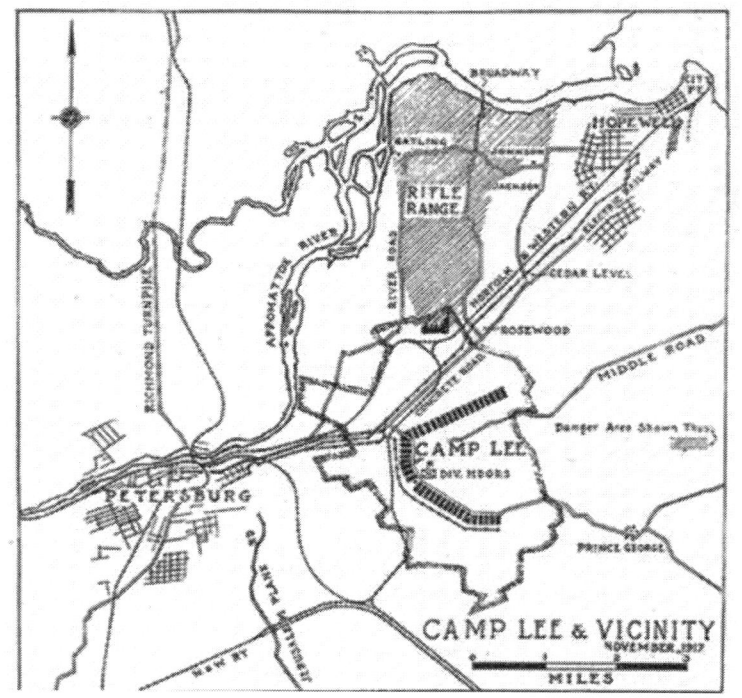

"Camp Lee and Vicinity." Camp Lee, where the 80th Division was assembled, is between Petersburg and Hopewell, Virginia. The camp itself is built in a giant "Horseshoe" pattern. Note the size of the camp's rifle range, which was constructed along the south bank of the Appomattox River.

The camp's and the division's H.Q. on Camp Lee: "The White House." It was one of the remaining farm houses of the site.

Close-up of "The White House," the H.Q. of Camp Lee and the 80th Division.

Two of the unsung heroes of the war: The intrepid Maj. Charles Sweeny (L), commander of 2/318th Inf. (later 1/318th Inf.) and Capt. John Crum, commander of F/318th Inf. at Camp Lee. They led us through thick and thin from beginning to end. A one-time a student at West Point, Sweeny served as a mercenary officer in Mexico and as a member of the French Foreign Legion, fighting in Flanders during our Great War. Rising from the ranks to captain, he was awarded the prestigious Legion of Honor. Once the U.S. declared war, he joined the U.S. Army as an infantry major. Crum had fought with Pancho Villa in Mexico and with the British in Flanders before he joined the regiment.

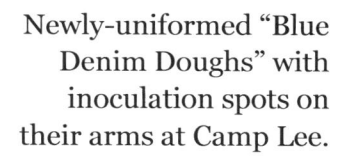

Newly-uniformed "Blue Denim Doughs" with inoculation spots on their arms at Camp Lee.

"Instructing the Latest Arrivals, Camp Lee."

80th Division recruits practice drill with wooden sticks rather than rifles at Camp Lee during the first few weeks of training. Until supplies of weapons and equipment arrived, instructors had to make do with substitutes. Constant drill taught teamwork and taught soldiers to respond quickly to orders.

K/3/317th Inf. recruits with old Krag-Springfield M1892s, used for training purposes during the first several weeks at Camp Lee.

Typical soldier pack with canvas pistol belt (L). We'd stuff our shelter half, three aluminum tent pins, three wooden tent poles, slicker, blanket, overcoat, and extra shirt, underwear, and socks into this pack, as well as a few personal and sundry items. School of the Squad, (R).

Typical company formation at Camp Lee.

Close order drill at Camp Lee.

With full pack, marching through Petersburg.

Some of the British (L) and French (R) instructors who
helped train us at Camp Lee, 1917-18.

Maréchal de France Joseph Joffre "Papa Joffre" (L), *Général de France* Charles Mangin "the Butcher" (C), and Maj. Gen. Robert Lee Bullard, commander, 1st Inf. Div. and III Corps, A.E.F. (R).

Two rifle squads from 319th Inf. at Camp Lee. They are armed with new M1917 Enfield Magazine Rifles. These are the rifles we took with us to France.

At the Camp Lee Rifle Range with M1917s.

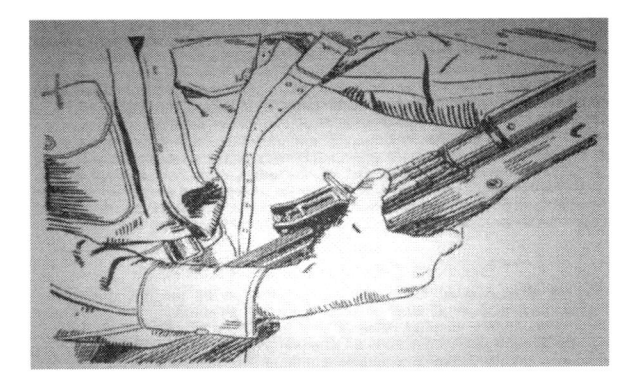

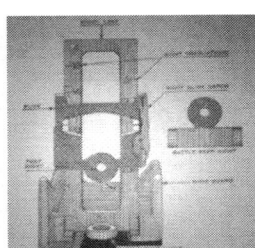

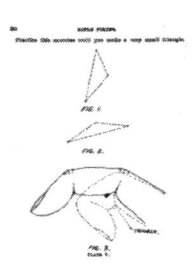

Proper sight picture on an M1917 (L), the rear sight aperature on an M1917 (C), and proper trigger squeeze (R).

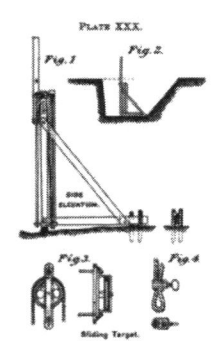

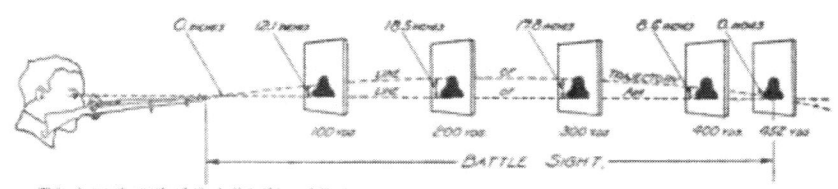

This shows the path of the bullet (Line of Trajectory) of the 1917 Rifle (Enfield).
The Line of Aim, we see, connects the eye, the rear sight, the front sight and the bottom part of the target. It is a straight line.
We see that the Line of Trajectory crosses the Line of Aim at two points. The distance between these points is 452 yards. Therefore, 452 yards is the Battle Sight Range for the 1917 Rifle.

THE BAYONET.

Nomenclature and Description.

11. The bayonet is a cutting and thrusting weapon consisting of three principal parts, viz. the *blade*, *guard*, and *grip*.

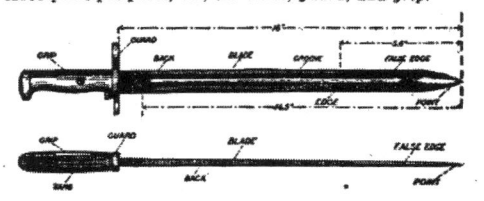

Par. 24. Par. 29. Par. 28.

Par. 40. Par. 41. Par. 42. Par. 44.

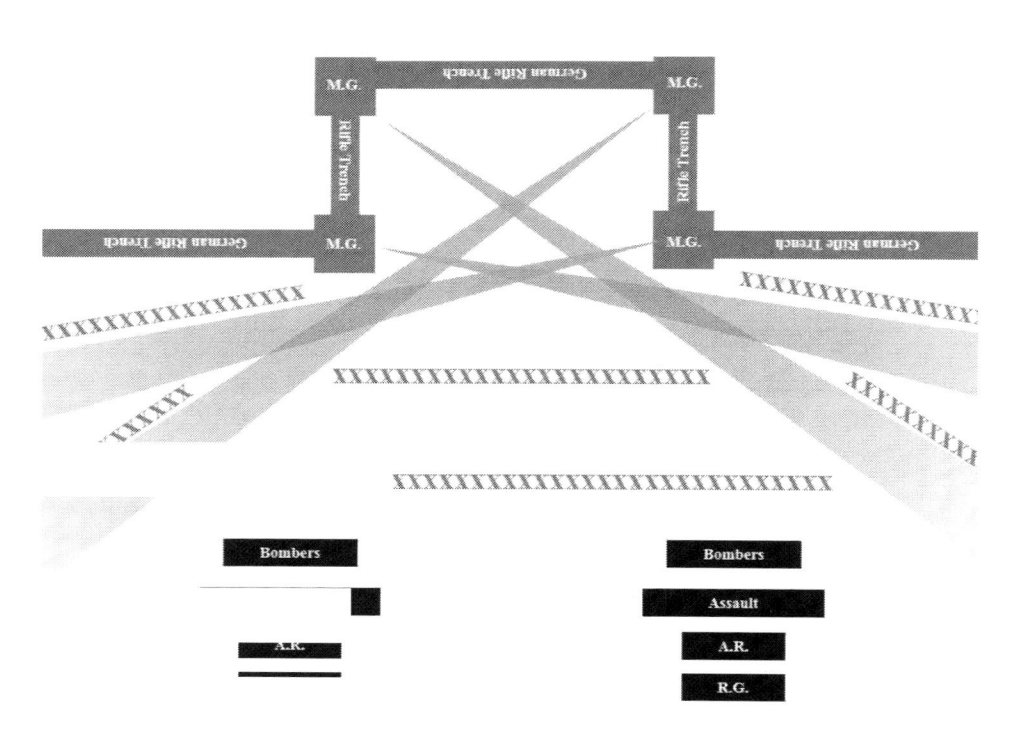

Basic platoon drill to take out German M.G. nests. As the dug-in M.G. nests were protected by interlocking fields of fire, getting shot from the flank or in enfilade, was our biggest concern. While the M.G.s fired up a line of barbed wire at an angle, squads of Hun infantry, armed with rifles and hand grenades, would usually fire straight on, protecting the flanks of the M.G.s. On the top, it shows how our infantry companies usually advanced in two platoon columns with squads stacked, one behind the other. On the bottom, as the bomber squad neared the target and were stopped by well-placed Hun M.G. fire, the A.R.s would maneuver and suppress the M.G.s to their right or left. Behind them would come the R.G.s, who would shoot W.P. smoke grenades at the M.G. nest embrasures.

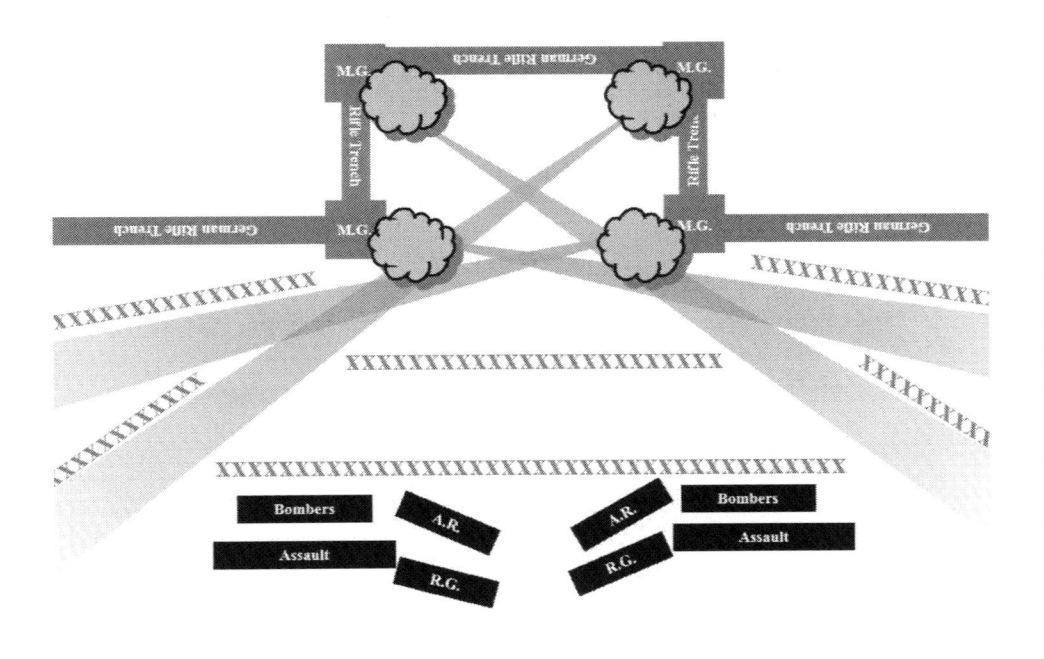

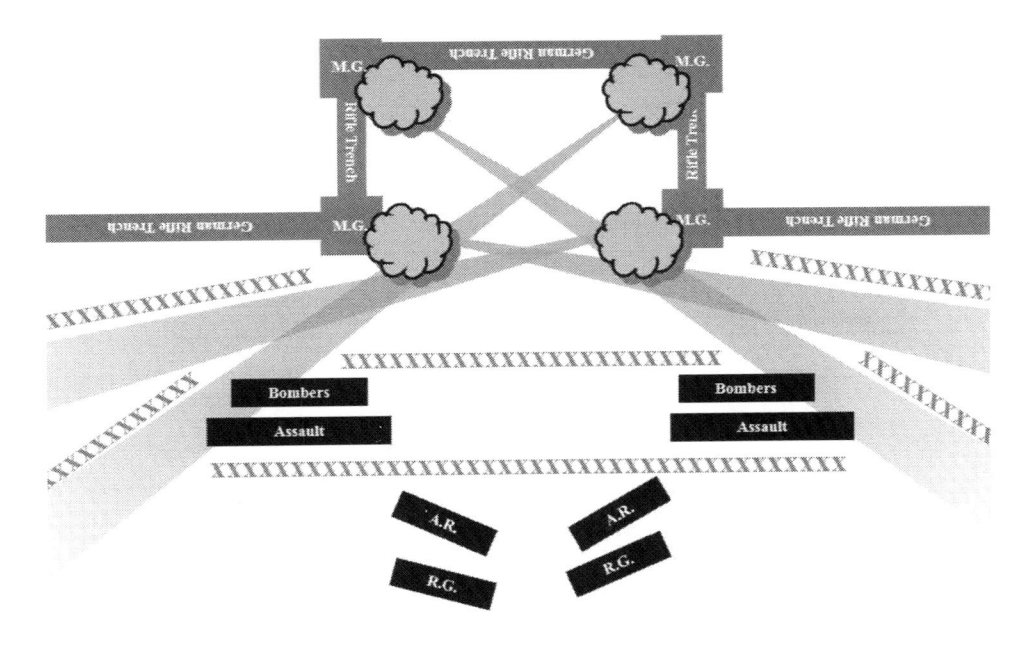

Basic platoon drill to take out German M.G. nests. As the dug-in M.G. nests were protected by interlocking fields of fire, getting shot from the flank or in enfilade, was our biggest concern. While the M.G.s fired up a line of barbed wire at an angle, squads of Hun infantry, armed with rifles and hand grenades, would usually fire straight on, protecting the flanks of the M.G.s. On the top, it shows how our infantry companies usually advanced in two platoon columns with squads stacked, one behind the other. On the bottom, as the bomber squad neared the target and were stopped by well-placed Hun M.G. fire, the A.R.s would maneuver and suppress the M.G.s to their right or left. Behind them would come the R.G.s, who would shoot W.P. smoke grenades at the M.G. nest embrasures.

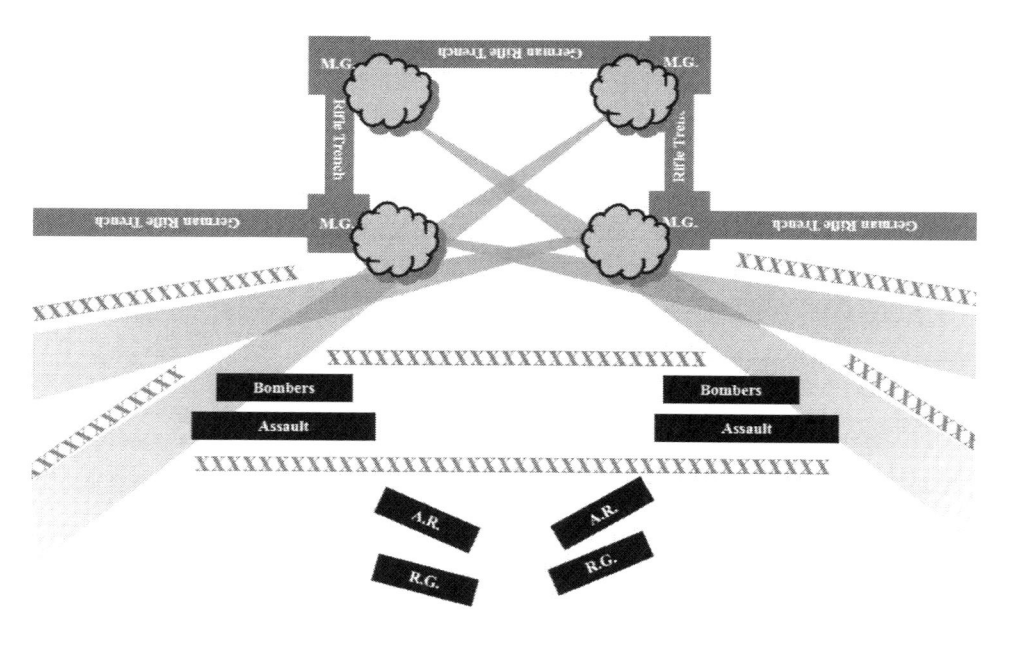

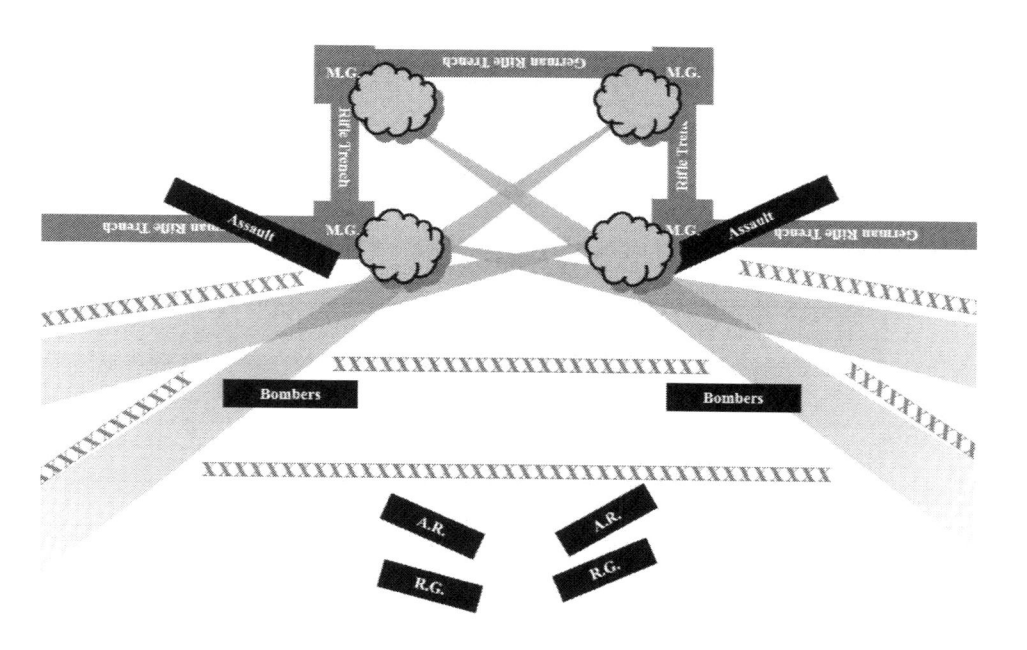

Gaining fire superirority was the key (top). If his platoon was not gaining it, the P.L. would send a patrol back to bring up an M1915 M.G. or an I.G. Once it was determined that the platoon had in fact achieved fire superiority, the P.L. would lead the assault squad through the bombers (bottom) and charge the enemy position, taking the Hun M.G. nest in flank and rear. Once the assault is launched, the P.G. would lead what was left of the bomber, the A.R., and R.G. squads to hold the position. Immediately behind these two platoons were two more platoons from the same company and behind them were four more platoons from another company in the same battalion. The key was to always keep the attack moving forward.

M1915 Colt-Vickers 30.06 cal. M.G.s that the 80th Division used during most of their combat operations in France. Note the condenser hose connected to the condenser box and that the piece loads from right to left.

Notice that we called the ammunition belt "The Kaiser's Necklace."

Infantry Gun (I.G.) dismounted (L) and mounted (R).

French air-cool Hotchkiss M.G. being used by American Doughs in another division (L) and one of the Ford "Specials" used by the 315th M.G. Battalion (Mot.) (R).

Each Infantry company had several "combat carts" (L) and the 313th and 314th M.G. Battalions, as well as the M.G. companies of the Infantry regiments, also had carts. We thus called those M.G. units the "Jackass Artillery" (R).

"Advance Assembled," *M.G.M.* (L). A Blue Ridge M.G. Section "Advancing By Parts." Note all of the ammunition cans being carried, the tripod on one soldier's shoulder, and the gun on the soldier third from the rear. They are advancing up the Meuse-Argonne, fall 1918.

Each company had a horse or mule-drawn field kitchen (L) and a "Water Buffalo" (R). These were the most cherished pieces of equipment for the Doughs.

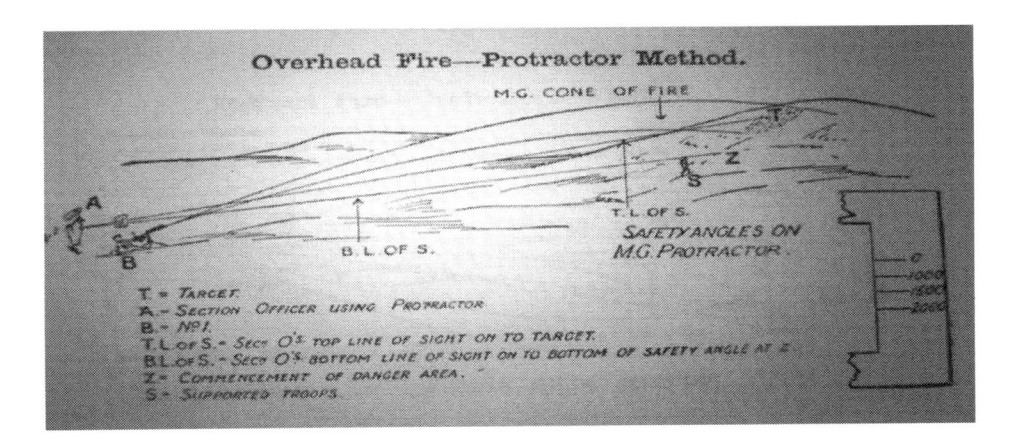

"Overhead Fire—Protractor Method." *B.M.G.M.*

Casualty Evacuation Carries. *M.S.T, 1917.*

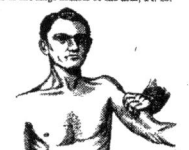

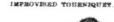

Litter training at Camp Lee, 1918.

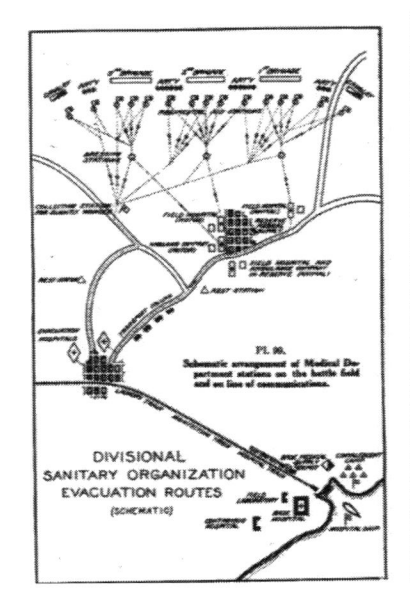

36

— and we gave
them hell —

Members of the 155th Arty. Brig. training on "Range Finders" at Camp Lee.

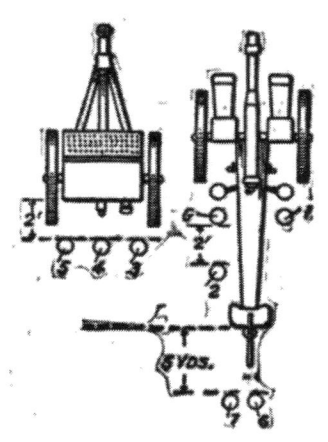

PLATE 41, Par. 188.

Gun Squad positions (left) and caisson, gun carriage, and caisson (below).

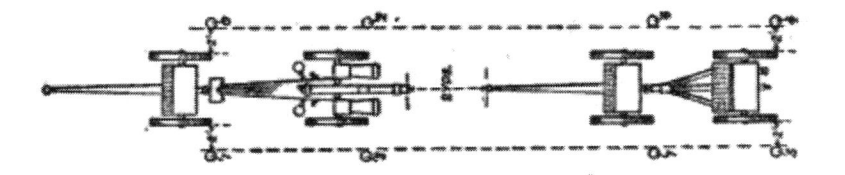

M1902 three-inch Field Gun. In France, the A.E.F. fired French 75mm field guns instead.

A French 75mm Field Gun going into battery.

M1908 6-inch Howitzer.

French *Schneider* 155mm Howitzer in action. The 315th Arty. would fire these monsters in France.

French *Schneider* 155mm Howitzer with limber in "travel lock" position.

Artillery training at Dutch Gap, Virginia, 1918.

Firing the M1902 three-inch Field Gun at Dutch Gap.

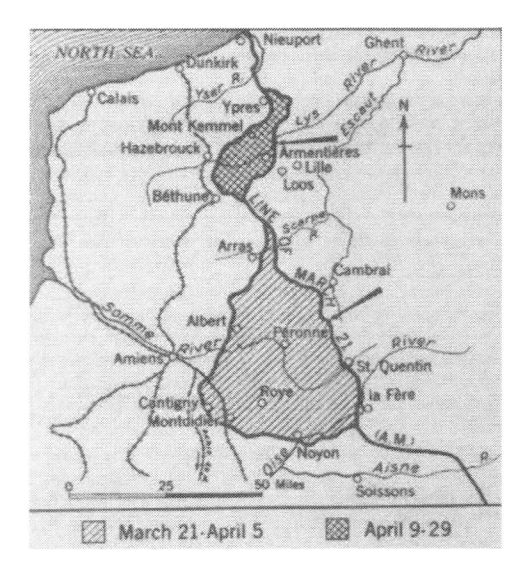

"Ground Gained by German Offensives of March and April, 1918, *A.B.M.C.* (L) and *Maréchal de France* Ferdinand Foch, Supreme Commander of Allied and Associated Forces (R).

German troops advance during *Friedensturm*.

Rear Admiral William S. Sims, Commander of the U.S. Atlantic Fleet in European Waters during the War (L) and Maj. Gen. Robert Lee Bullard, commander, 1st Inf. Div. and later the American III Corps (R).

"Loading 160th Inf. Bde. troops for France on the James, City Point, Va., 5-25-18."

"Leaving Newport News with Brett's 160th Inf. Brig." (L) and "U.S. Destroyer at Sea 6-7-18. Our convoy to France. Protection to 13 transports." This would have been the U.S.S. *Huntington*, which escorted the 160th Inf. Bde.

U.S.S. *Siboney*, which transported the 313th Arty. and the 305th Ammunition, Supply, and Transportation Trains from Norfolk to Brest (L) and a typical American convoy headed across the North Atlantic to France, 1918 (R).

Hello France! Brest Harbor with the 319th Inf. (L) and "Disembarkation in France." We wore our M1911 Campaign Hats well into the summer, until we received M1917 Overseas Service Caps (R).

"Newly Arrived Troops Disembarking at Brest" by Jack Duncan.

"Mess call at camp in Brest, 6-10-18."

Army logistical zones in France. The main ports of debarkation for the Doughboys were Brest, St. Nazaire, or Bordeaux. The main A.E.F. supply line ran from Brest to Chaumont, where Pershing's H.Q. was located.

319th Inf. soldiers on their way to Calais, June 14, 1918.

Views of Camp Pontanzen, France.

40 or 8s.

"Good-Bye Calais—A car load of Hommes." Blue Ridgers on a 40 or 8.

Front lines and "Areas of Interest of the 80th Division." *A.B.M.C.* During Friedensturm, the Germans were looking to drive up the Somme River Valley and drive the British from the continent.

Bell-shaped tents at "Rest Camp No. 6" near Calais.

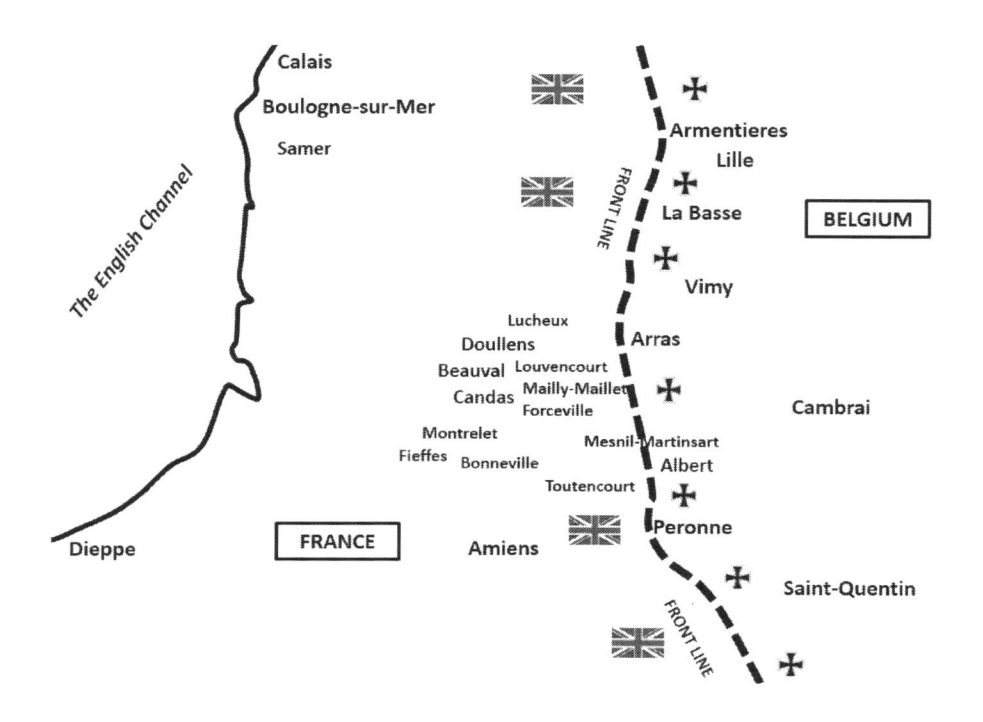

Training with the Tommies in Picardy.

Washing day (L) and platoon leaders censoring letters (R).

Sharpening bayonets (L) and "80th Division Reconnaissance Car" is representative of the many types of vehicles the division fielded in France. We generally called them "Specials."

Standard gear of a Doughboy in France. This soldier is armed with an Enfield Rifle and carris a British respirator bag. Across the top of his pack is an extra blanket. On his pack he carries his anti-shrapnel helmet and beheath it is his intrenching tool.

An 80th Division signal station in action (L). Comunications are key to victory in modern war: "The fustest with the mostest." A Dough Boy with a Y.M.C.A. doughnut (R). And no, we were not called "Doughboys" because of the donuts (as far as I know).

British Maj. Gen. Julian Byng commanded the British Third Army in Picardy. The 80th Division was attached to his command and participated in the Somme Offensive, 1918.

"A camouflaged camp in the front lines one mile from Albert, 7-26-18."

French Rifle Grenade "Tromblon" trainer (L) and the tromblons used in action (R).

French "*Renault*" F.T. light or "Mosquito" tank (L) and a French "*Schneider*" medium tank (R).

French *Saint-Chamond* heavy tank (L) and British Mark V heavy tank.

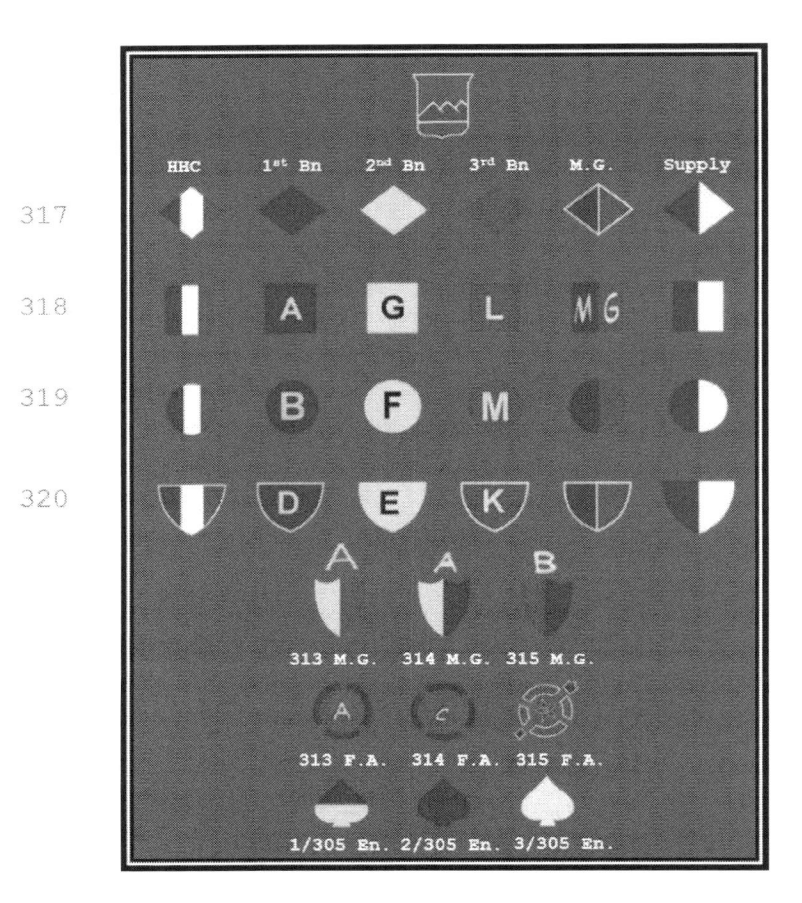

80th Division battalion designs that were painted on our helmets. The infantry regiments are along the top, followed by the M.G. battalions, the artillery regiments, and then the engineer battalions.

Resperator bag of J.C. Wisinger. The designs denote that he was a member of 3/305 Engineers, 80th Division.

50

Rolling to Picardy in a 40 or 8. High living!

The 320th Infantry disembarks in Picardy to fight alongside Byng's British army.

"Old Virginia Never Tires" placard attached to one of our Supply/318th Infantry wagons. Each Infantry regiment had scores of this type of G.S. wagon.

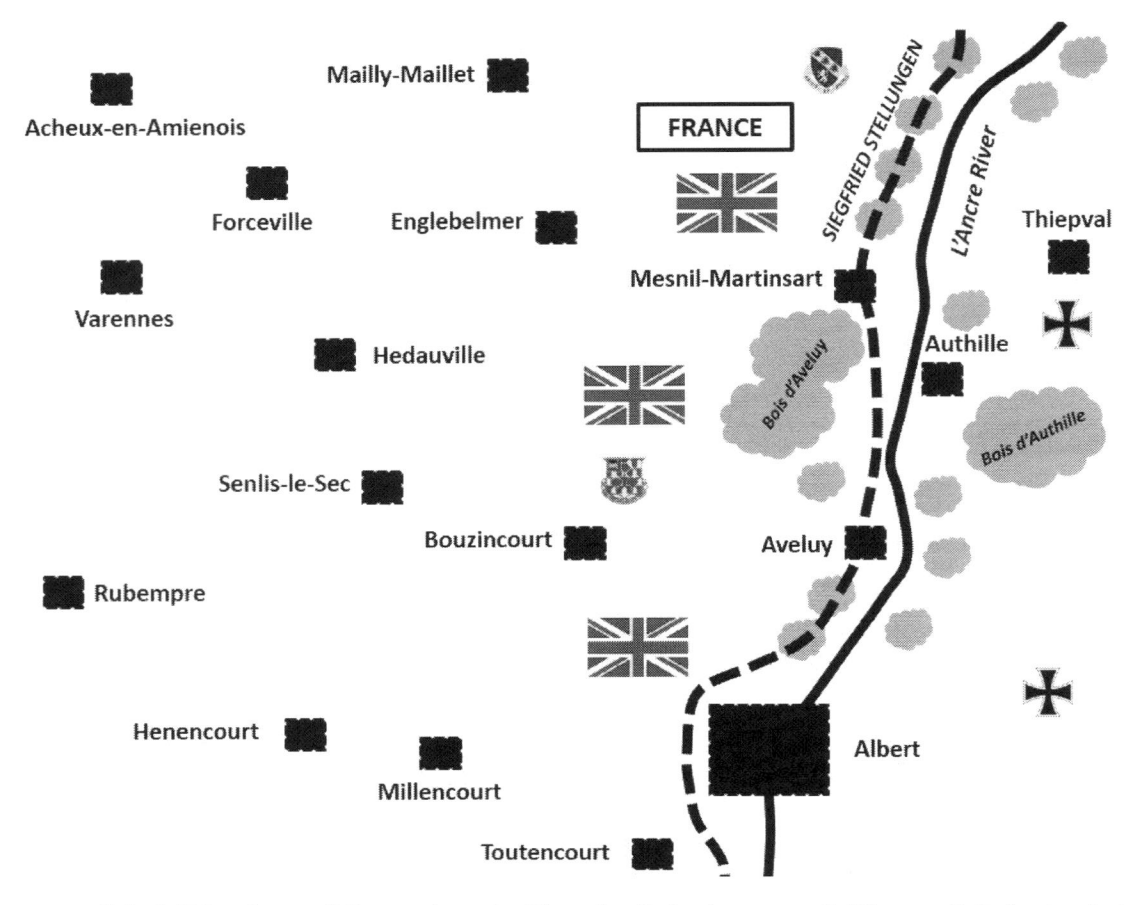

159th Inf. Bde. Area of Operations in Picardy, July-Aug., 1918. The 317th Infantry is in the north and the 318th Infantry is in the south.

"From the top of this hill we could see our shells exploding in the German lines. 7-22-18." Looking across the flat and fat farmland-turned-battlefield of northern France (L) and the Ancre River, just north of Albert (R).

"Over the Top" by J. Andre Smith. This is what it was like along the Green or "Outpost Line."

"Chateau Henencourt: A half mile from the Jerry lines in the Arras Sector near Albert."

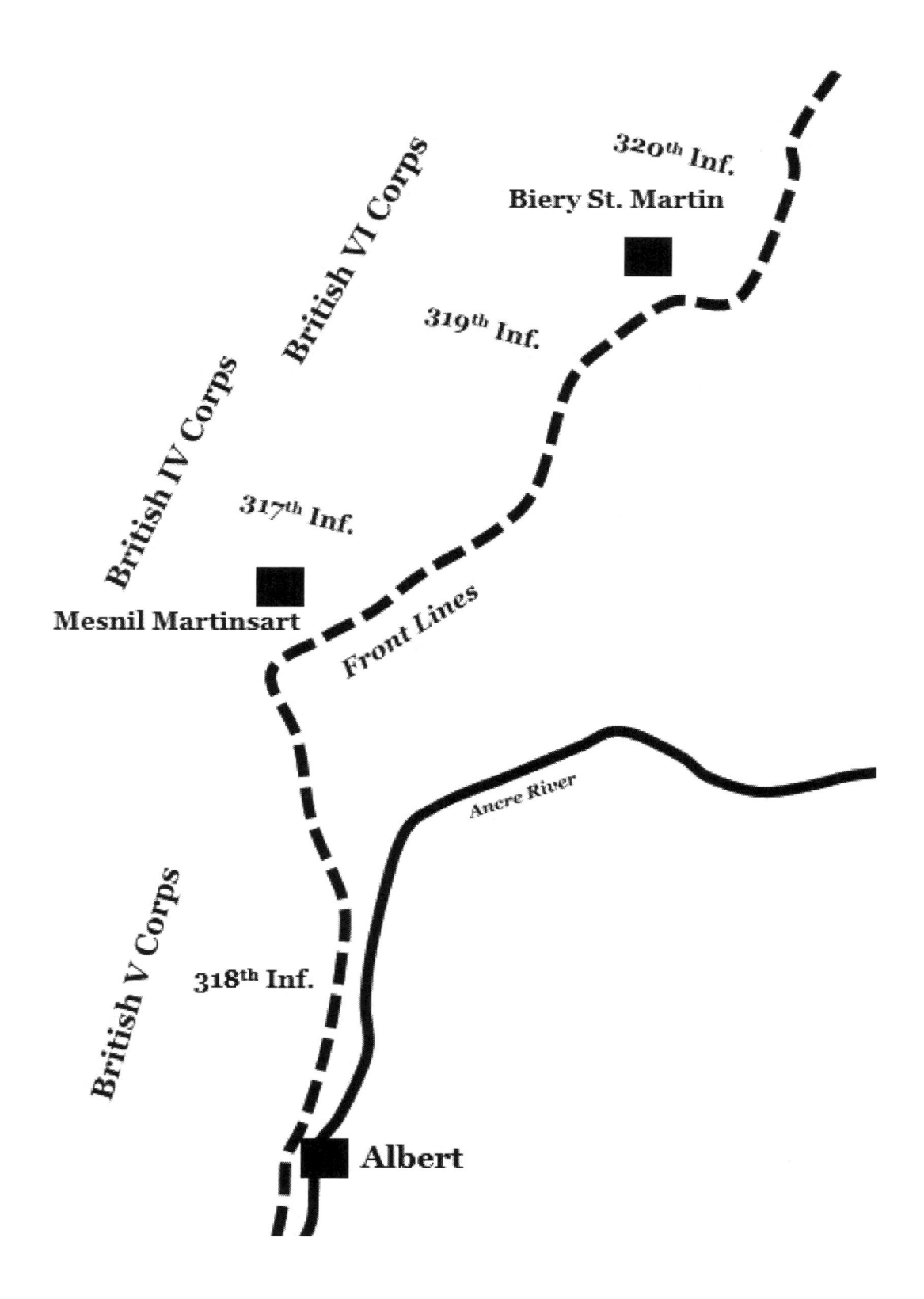

80th Division positions "Up the Line" with Byng's British Third Army at Albert, France, Aug., 1918.

When firing the M1915 Chauchat Automatic Rifle from a fixed position, we would drop the bi-pod. Note the "banana" magazine for the bullets. On the right is a Dough Automatic Rifle team, just like Getz and I.

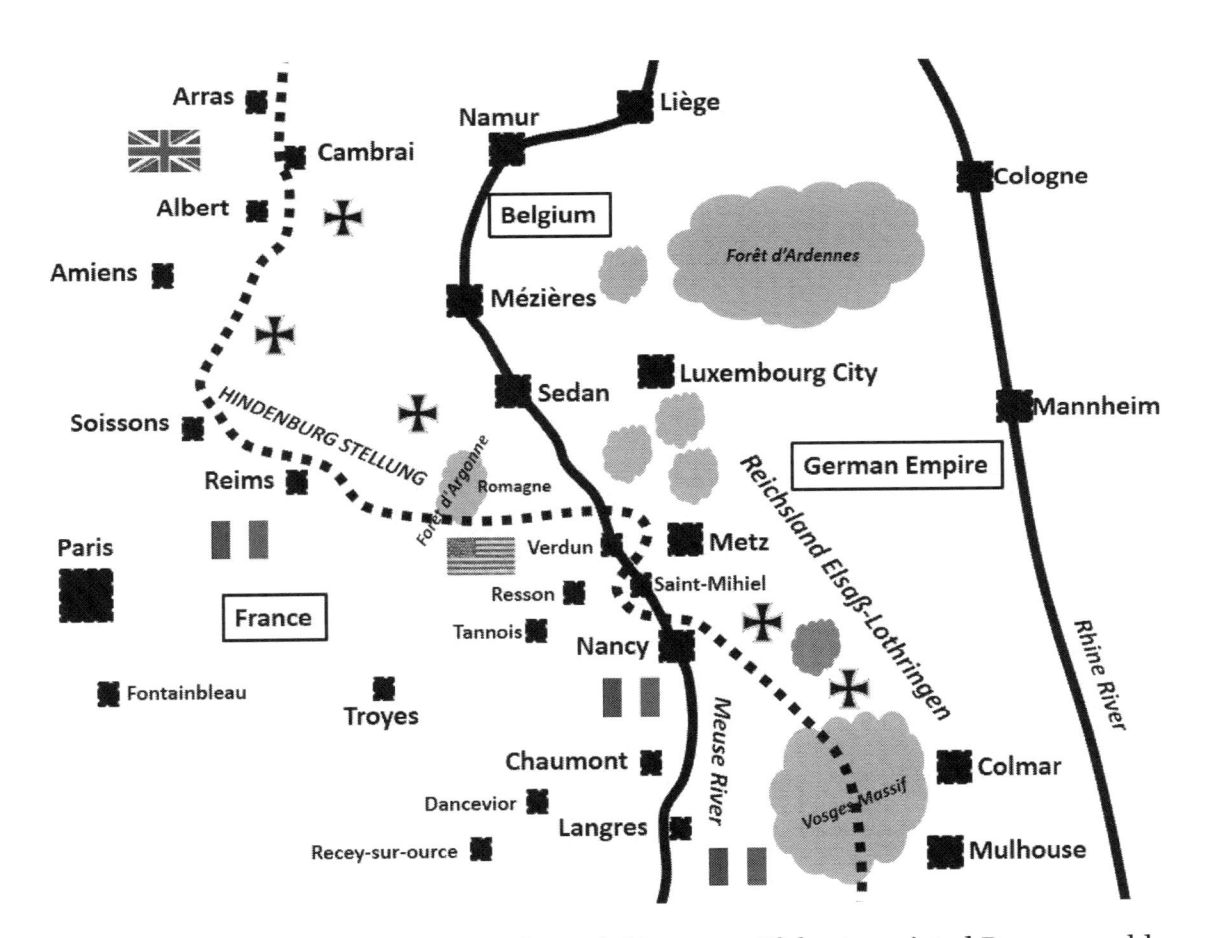

80th Inf. Div. Area of Operations, July 1918-May 1919. If the Associated Powers could break through at Romagne in the Meuse-Argonne and take Sedan and Mézières, they could turn the Germans from their position in France and Belgium.

"Dugout—Senlis. A Yank Home on the front lines." 319th Inf. in camp, 1918.

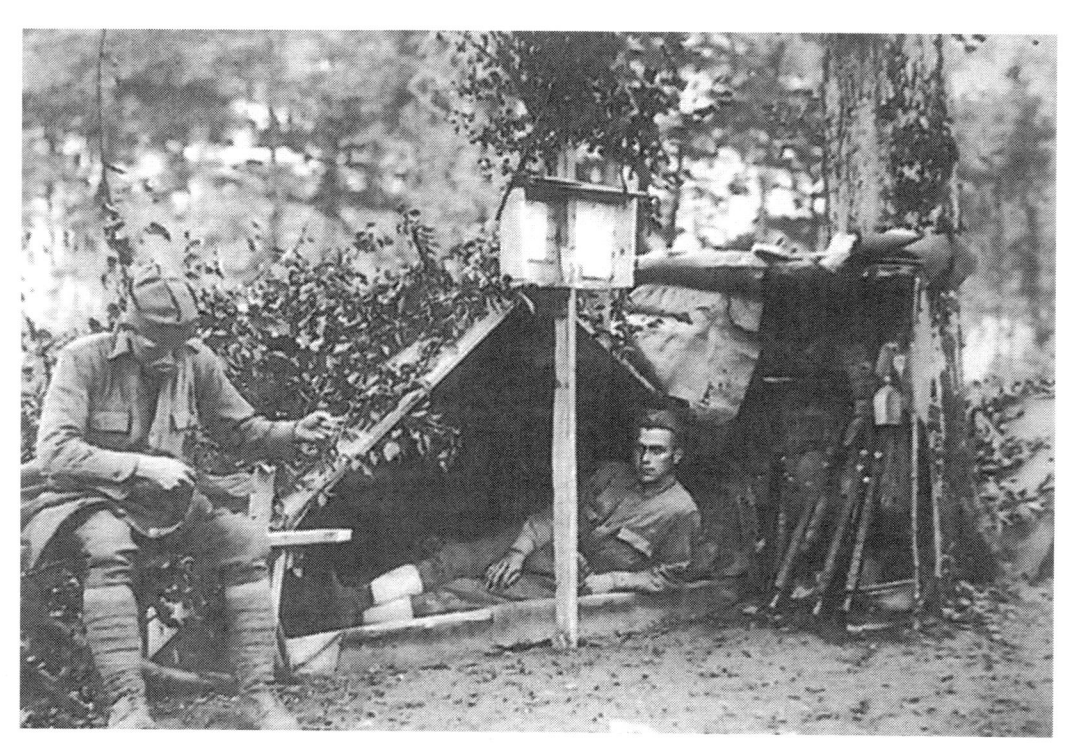

80th Division Doughs in camp, August, 1918.

"Home Sweet Home
Up the Line."

Camions to the front.

An 81mm British Stokes Mortar. Each Inf. regiment had
at least two.

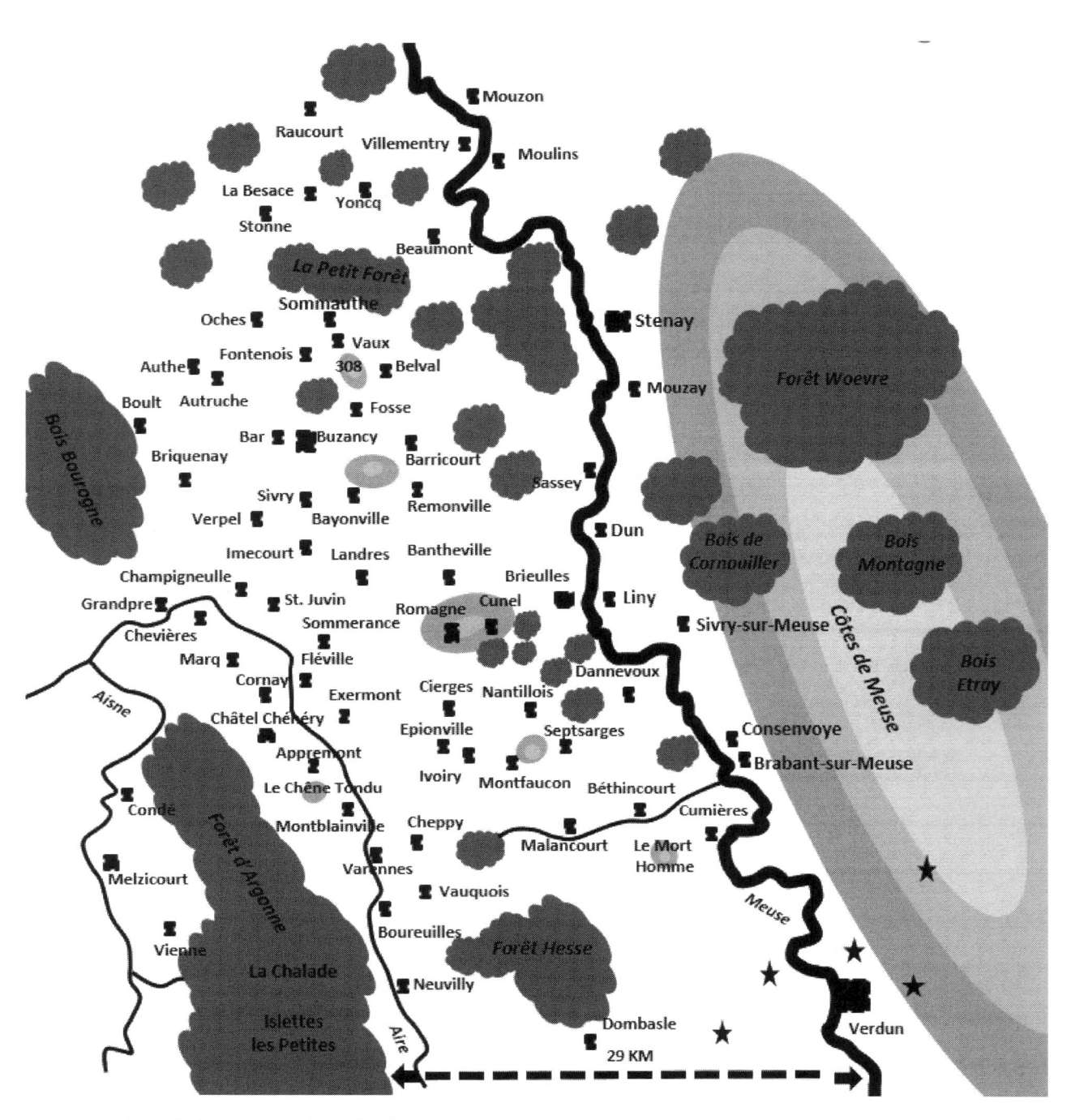

80th Division Operations in the Meuse Argonne, Sept.-Nov., 1918. The Meuse River is on the right and the Argonne Forest is on the left. The division mostly operated in the vicinity of Béthincourt, Septsarges, Dannevoux, Nantillois, Cunel, Sommerance, Immecourt, Sivry, Buzancy, Sommauthe, and Yoncq. The *Bois d' Ogons* is between Nantillois and Cunel in the center of the sector.

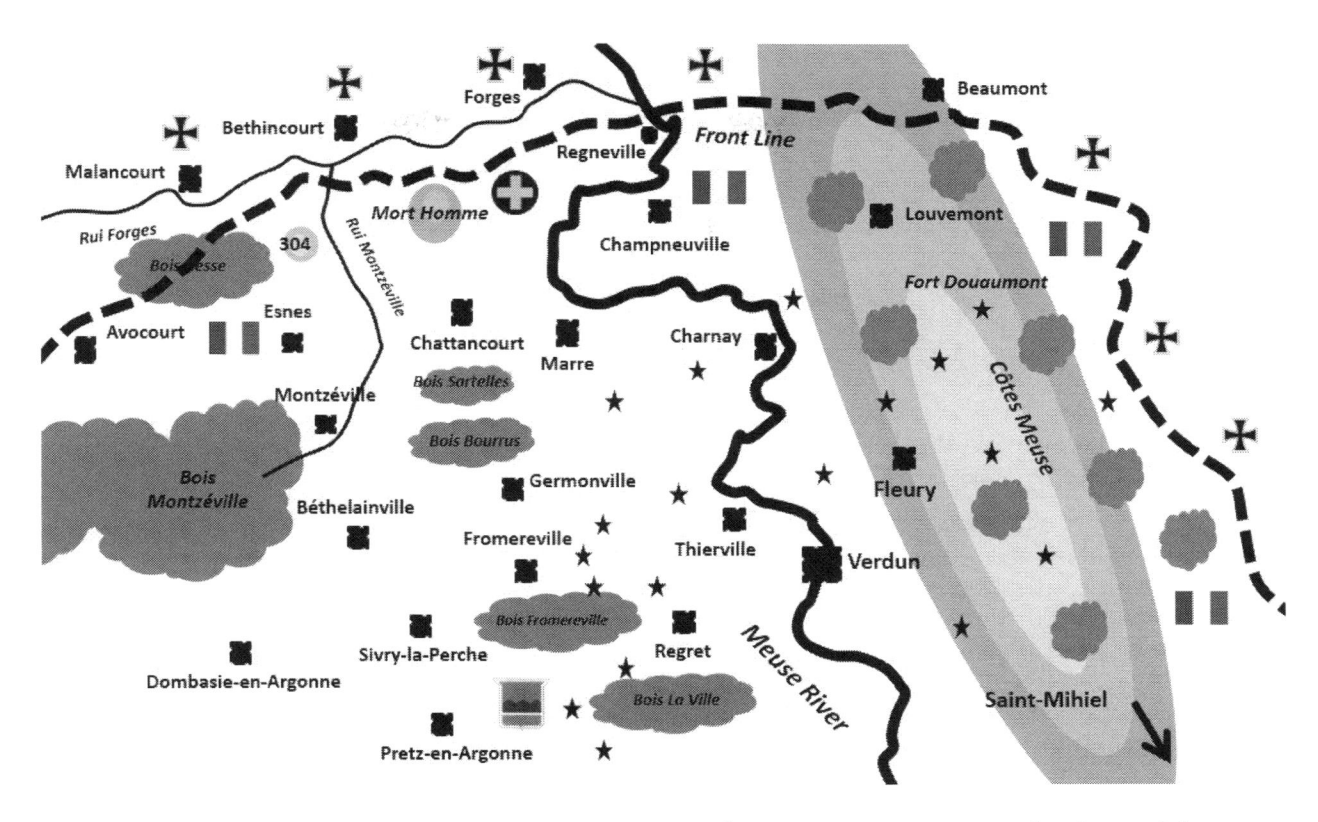

Advance to the Meuse-Argonne Sept. 16-25, 1918. The star icons represent the forts of the area.

"Barber Shop and a dug-out in the front lines 9-11-18" (L) and "Water Cart near Germonville, 9-25-18." This company water buffalo is being filled by a Q.M. water tanker (R).

"The gate at Verdun" is said to have been the inspiration for the insignia of the U.S. Corps of Engineers (L) and *Général de France* Robert Nivelle, the man who famously coined the phrase at Verdun: "They shall not pass!" (R) He also infamously led the abortive 1917 "Nivelle Offensive" which drove much of the once-proud French Army to mutiny. Pershing argued that if we would have sent 500,000 trained Americans to France in 1917, the British and French may have broken through.

German *General der Artillerie* Max Karl Wilhelm von Gallwitz, Pershing's opposite in the Meuse-Argonne (L) and "Field apothecary, 317th Inf., 80th Div., Sept. 19, 1918" (R).

Riding in the back of a steel-wheeled *camion* was not easy (L) and engineers working on a road in the muddy Meuse-Argonne Sector (R).

"On the War Path" with the 318th Inf. (L) and "American Troops Passing Through Chattancourt" (R).

"Road Scene at Esnes, an Important Road Center During the Meuse Argonne Operation" (L) and French "Hairy Ones" in the trenches of the Meuse-Argonne (R).

Blue Ridge P.C. in the Meuse-Argonne (L) and Brig. Gen. Fox Connor, Pershing's Operations Officer. "The Man Behind the Curtain" at the Meuse-Argonne (R).

Blue Ridge Infantry Division Doughs advancing "Up the Line" in the Meuse-Argonne.

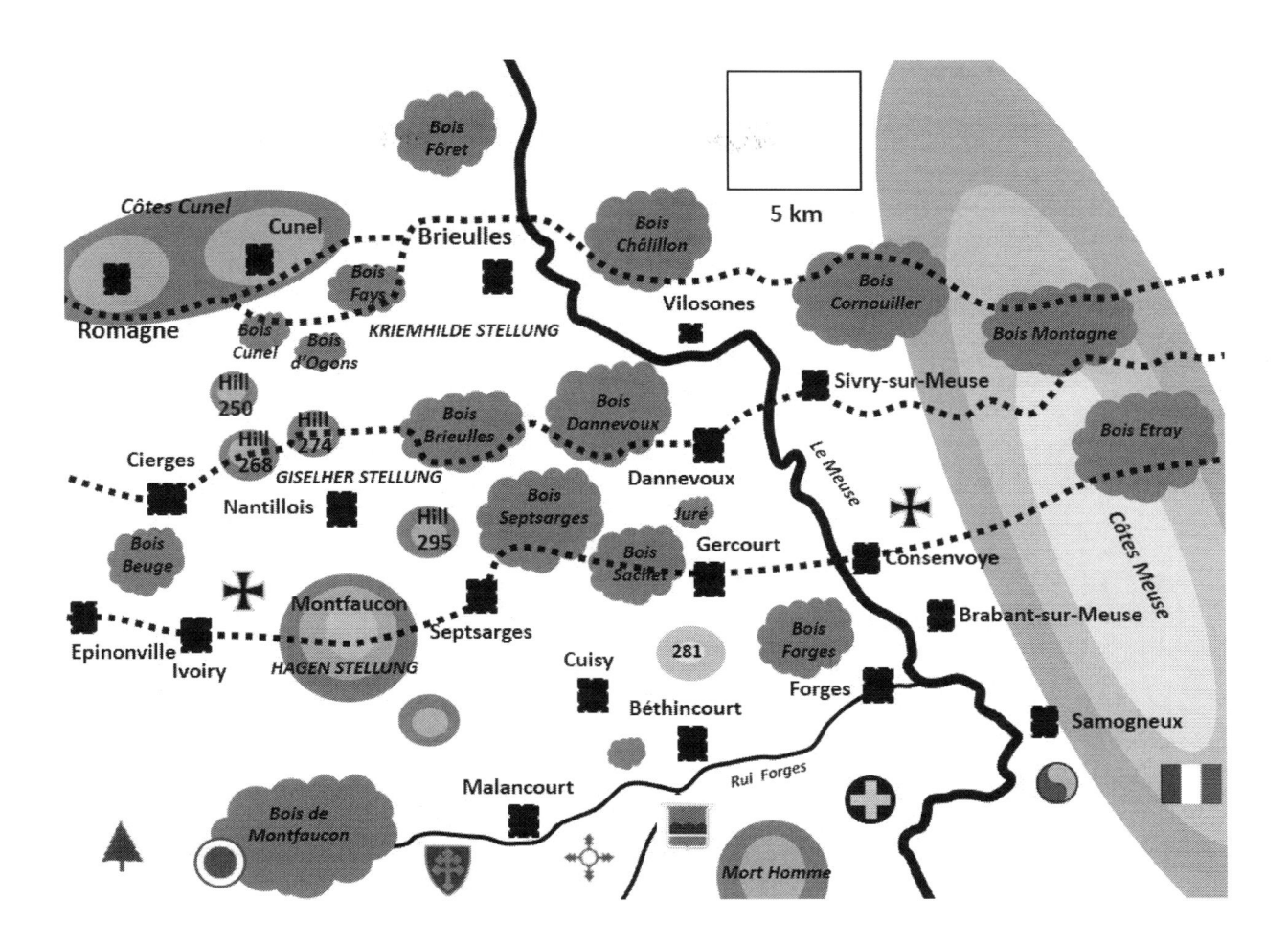

The eastern half of the Meuse-Argonne sector, Sept. 24, 1918. The 80th Division's axis of advance: Béthincourt-Gercourt-Dannevoux.

Engineers working on a road in the Meuse-Argonne Sector (L) and Maj. Gen. Robert Lee Bullard, Commander, American III Corps (R).

Gun squad from the 313th Arty. "in readiness." Note how the crew has used tree limbs to help camouflage the guns from aerial observation.

"Camouflaged Road Near Forges" (L) and the forward lines just south of Forges Creek. We were actually quite surprised by how primitive the forward trenches were in this zone.

Doughs from the 160th Inf. Brig. assemble near Forges Creek, Sept. 25, 1918.

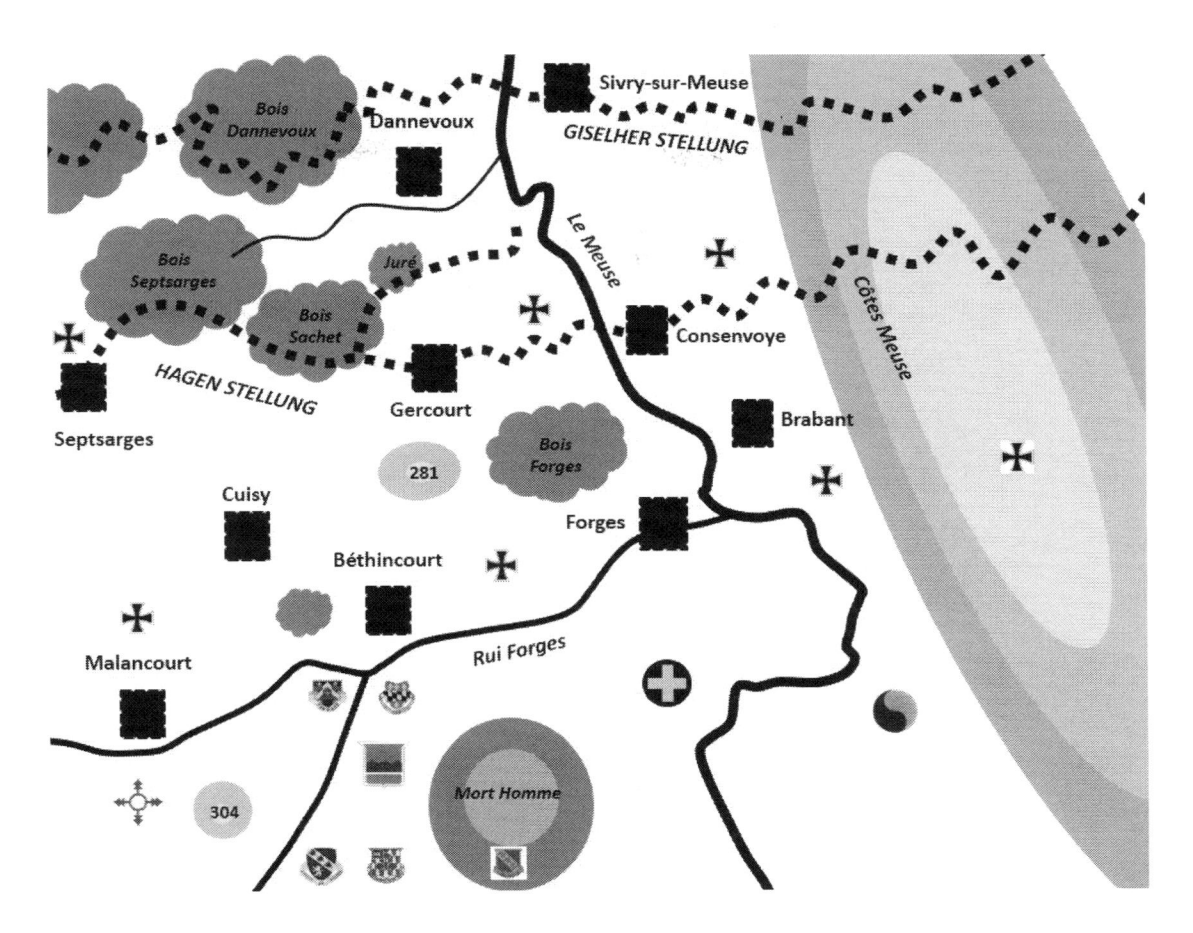

80th Inf. Div. Area of Operations, Sept. 26, 1918, dawn. The 320th Inf. is on the left and the 319th Inf. is on the right. The Artillery of the division is deployed between Mort Homme and Hill 304.

What we had to fight through. The little dots in the ditches on the left were us.

The M1917 French Schneider 155mm Howitzer was used in place of the U.S. M1908 6-inch Howitzer in France (L). It is posted "in immediate action, in the open" (L) and 155mm howitzers firing in the Meuse-Argonne (R). The 315th Arty. was armed with these types of howitzers. These guns are posted "in observation, masked" (R).

Looking north—attack axis of the 319th Inf. The Hun with the Gun were dug-in deep along the ridge line. Note the wide open fields of fire—a defender's dream.

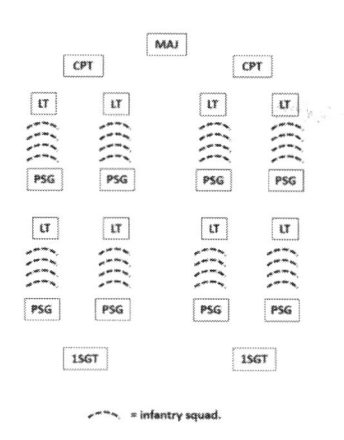

Conceptual sketch (L) of lead companies in an attack battalion, Sept. 26, 1918. Because this was a breaching operation, we attacked in depth along a narrow front and (R) "Ruins of Bèthincourt, 9-26-18; held by the Germans and captured by the Yanks in the Argonne Offensive" (R).

"'H' Hour troops at the Forges River at daybreak. Jumping off place of the Argonne Drive. Company 'B' Bridge. Bethincourt, 9-26-18" (L). These troops were from B/1/305th En. and the 160th Inf. Brig. "Company 'B' Bridge at Bethincourt, 9-26-18. Bridge over the Forges River constructed by the 305th Engrs. while under shell fire" (R). Shown is a caisson squad from one of the light batteries of the division.

A gun from Capt. Perriman's C/1/313th Artillery crossing the "Engineer Bridge" at Béthincourt Sept. 26, 1917.

Hun outpost M.G. team (L). This is what the combat groups of the 160th Inf. Brig. dealt with in the early phase of the offensive. "German inf. firing with telescopic sights" (R).

"Toll of one shell: 14 horses and one man killed by one shell; Bethincourt, 10-2-18" (L) and Doughs advance through German lines in the Meuse-Argonne (R).

While R.G.ers lay down smoke and A.R.men suppress Hun M.G. nest embrasures, bombers throw their hand grenades at the targeted M.G. nest and the assault squad over-runs the position. Most of the time A.R.-men had to kneel in order to better suppress the target.

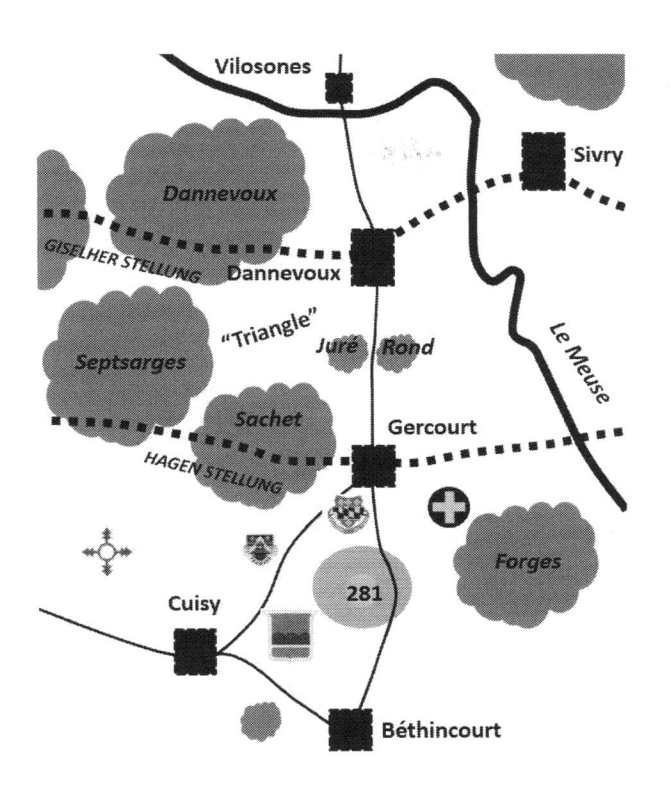

80th Inf. Div. Area of Operations, Sept. 26, 1918, Noon. The Yellow Cross icon represents the 33rd Division and the circle with four lines represents the 4th (Ivy) Division. The 319th Inf. attacked up the right and the 320th Infantry attacked up the left of the 80th Division axis of advance toward Dannevoux.

"Jerry Guns. Part of the 5,000 captured. Béthincourt 9-28-18."

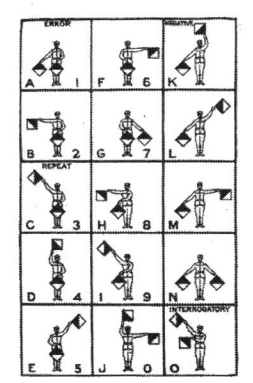

Dough Litter Team in action (L). The Litter Teams of the 319th Inf. transported men south through Gercourt. Semaphore Wig-Wag Signals (R). Note that some of the letters also meant things like "Error" or "Negative."

80th Inf. Div. Area of Operations, Sept. 26, 1918, 5:00 P.M. (right) and "Mopping Up Cierges" by Wallace Morgan (below). This captures what it was like for the 319th Inf. as it pushed through Gercourt and Dannevoux on Sept. 26, 1918.

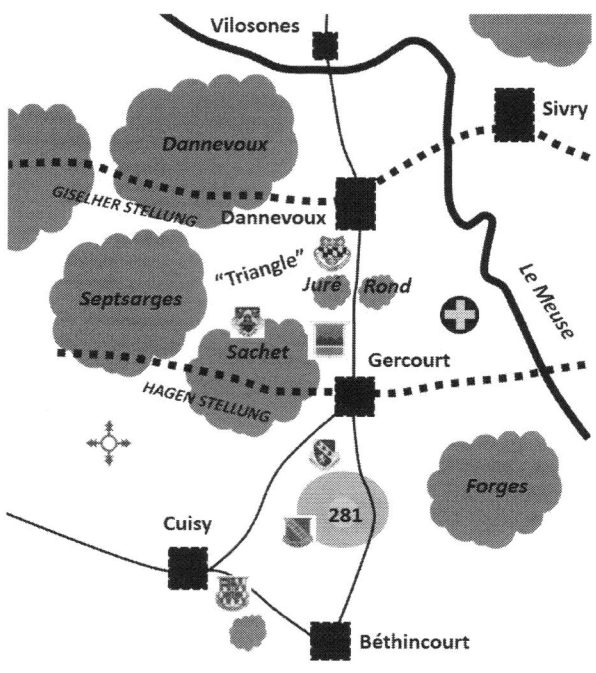

Typical Hun wire entanglements and trench works along *GISELHER*. Note the beautiful (and deadly) fields of fire.

Looking north into Dannevoux (L). The 319th Inf. attacked up this road and took the village on the evening of Sept. 26, 1918. *GISELHER* was along the ridge in the background. Looking northwest into Côtes Dannevoux (R) where the 319th and 320th Inf. Regts. adjoined and where *GISELHER* was situated.

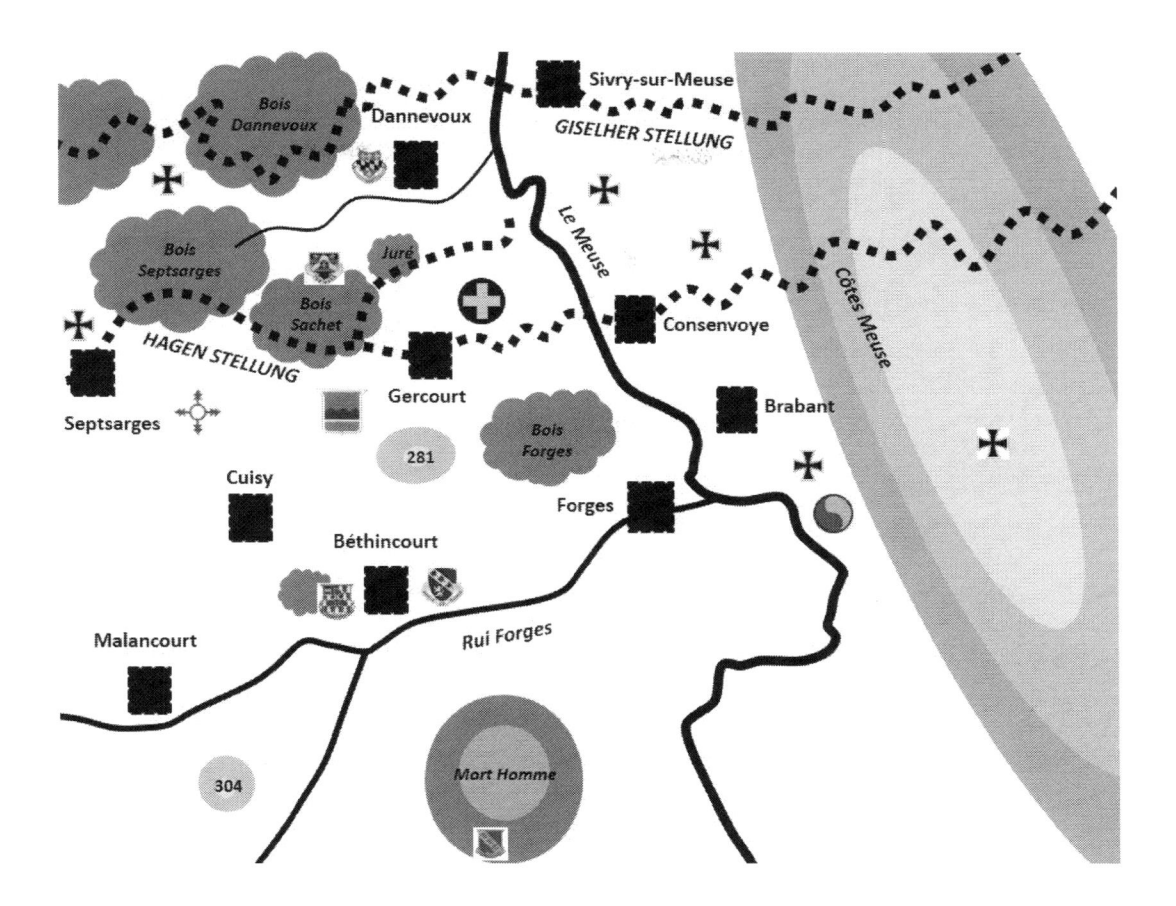

80th Inf. Div. Area of Operations, Sept. 26, 1918, 10:00 P.M. The swirl icon on the right represents the American 29th Division. In the 80th Division's zone, the 319th Inf. is in and around Dannevoux, the 320th Inf. is in Bois Sachet, the 317th and 318th Inf. Regts. of the 159th Inf. Brig. are around Béthincourt, and the division's 155th Artillery Brigade is massed between Mort Homme and Hill 304.

(L) Looking east—the 319th Inf. attacked from right to left. *Dannevoux is* in the center and *Côtes Meuse* is in the background. (R) looking south from *GISELHER*. The 319th Inf. attacked from the background and into the foreground on the first day of the Meuse-Argonne Offensive. Dannevoux is on the left and Bois Juré is on right.

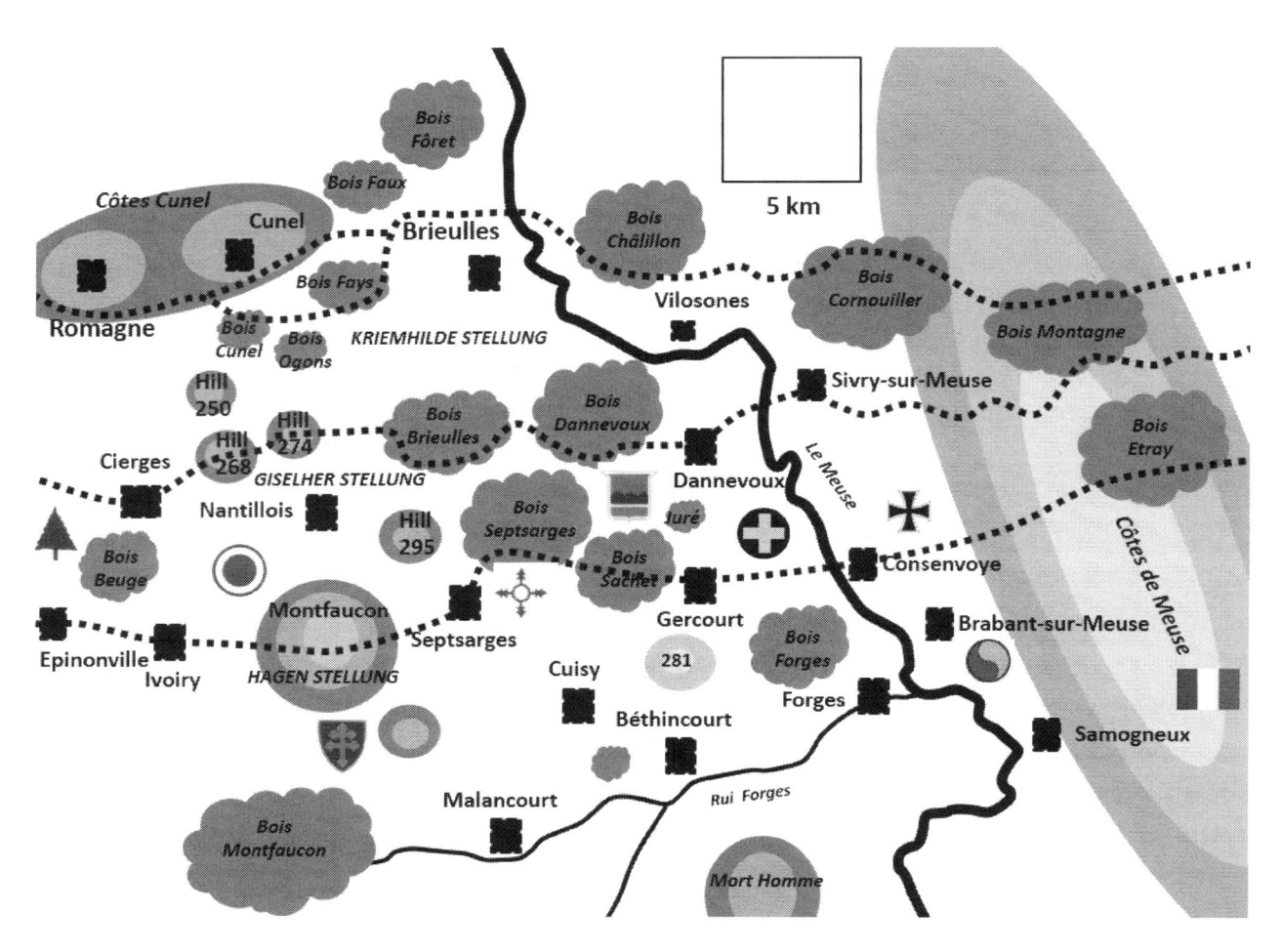

80th Inf. Div. Area of Operations, Sept. 27, 1918. While the 33rd (Prairie) and 80th (Blue Ridge) Divisions were to hold the right, the 4th (Ivy) and 37th (Buckeye) Divisions were to conduct a double-envelopment against Montfaucon on the left. The 79th (Cross of Lorraine) Division was still hung-up in front of Montfaucon, the lynch-pin of the German defenses in the area.

"Transport Congestion" at Hill 304, *Béthincourt*, Sept. 27, 1918" on (L) and "Moving Forward Up the Meuse-Argonne" on (R).

In destroyed villes like this (L), the Hun would turn into company strong points, backed by M.G.s. "No Man's Land south of Malancourt" (R).

"Nine km in two days. This was the advance made by the 80th Div. after the jump-off in the Meuse-Argonne beginning Sept. 26. Here are seen the commanding general of the division, Maj. Gen. Adelbert Cronkhite, and Col. William H. Waldron, his Chief of Staff. They are examining a map of the sector on their front." The picture on the right shows Brig. Gen. George Jamerson (second from L), commander of the 159th Inf. Brig., confers with Maj. Gen. Cronkhite (second from R).

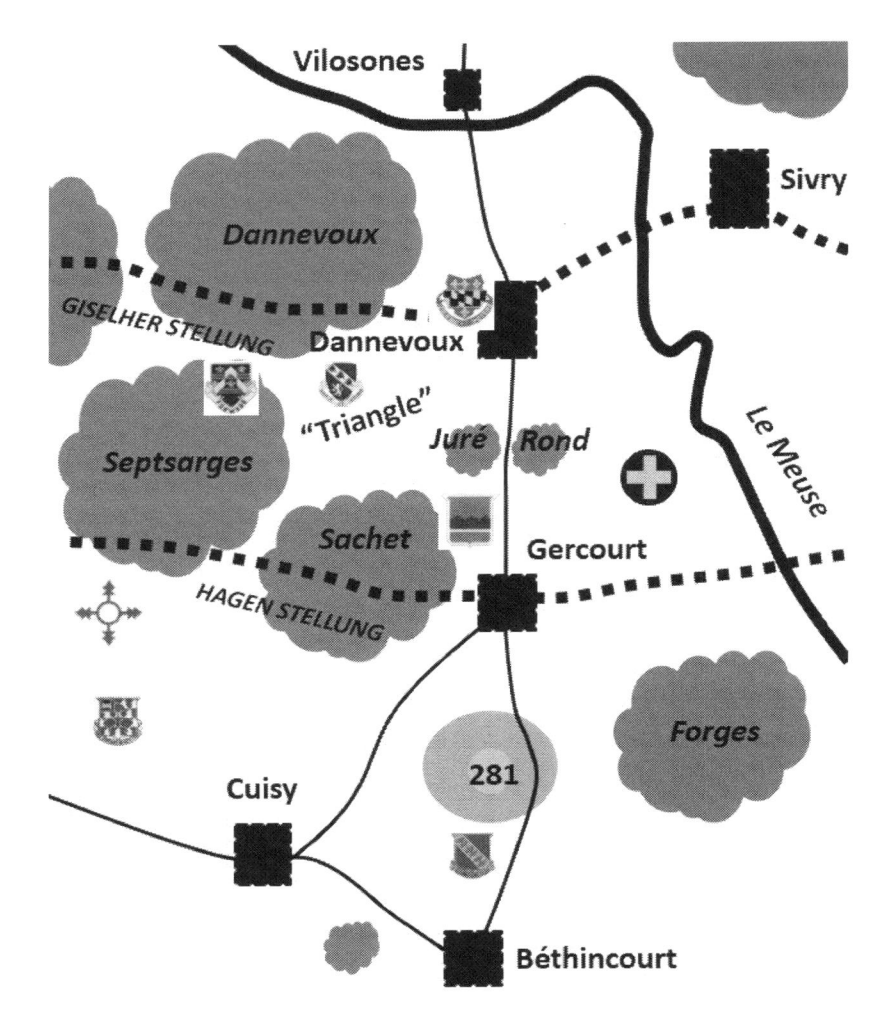

80th Inf. Div. Area of Operations, Sept. 27, 1918. While the 317th Inf. moved forward to support the 319th and 320th Inf. Regts., the 318th Inf. moved left to support the 4th "Ivy Division." The 155th Arty. Brig. was massed behind Hill 281 and between Cuisy and Béthincourt.

317th Inf. Mortar team at rest near Bois Brieulles (L). *Generalfeldmarschall* Paul von Hindenburg, *der Kaiser*, and *General der Infantrie* (lt. gen.) Erich von Ludendorff (R).

"Camouflaged guns in the foreground at Montfaucon, Sept. 28, 1918" (L) and "French tank. Montfaucon, 9-28-18. Going into action north of Septsarges." This is a French *Schneider* medium tank (R). Of all the tanks I saw, this was my favorite design.

"American Wounded Making Way to Aid Station" by George Matthews Harding (L) and "American Plane, Gercourt. One of the first to come down in the Meuse-Argonne, 9-28-18" (R). The areoplanes were so flimsy that we called them "motorized kites."

"Ruins of Montfaucon" (L) and "Decorations of the U.S.A."
A.B.M.C.

317th M.G. Section "Advaning in Parts" north through Bois Sachet.

Looking east across *GISELHER* into the Valley of the Meuse and the Heights of the Meuse (background). *Village Dannevoux* is off the picture to the right. This is near where 1/A/313th Arty. engaged Hun targets across the river on Sept. 27 (L) and "Looking north up the Valley of the Meuse" (R). In this vicinity, units from the 319th Inf. and the 313th Arty. engaged targets on *les Côtes Meuse*. In this area, the Germans had a communication bridge that they destroyed on the evening of Sept. 26, 1918.

314th Arty. "Guns in Observation" (L) and German Chancellor Friedrich Ebert of the Social Democratic Party (S.P.D.) of Germany (R).

Blue Ridgers moving through Montfaucon (L) and "Moving Up" (R).

Moving "Up the Line." A motor ambulance is in the background (L) and "Overhead View of Nantillois," looking east (R).

Poor *Nantillois* (L) and Light arty. moving north (R).

Waiting in a ditch for the next attack (L) and advancing up our axis of advance in the Meuse-Argonne (R).

Platoon from the 318th Inf. advancing under the cover of smoke in the Meuse-Argonne.

Maj. Gen. Adelbert Cronkhite (L). "The Hun." The average Prussian or Bavarian soldier we fought in the Meuse-Argonne looked like this. He was armed with a 7mm K98, several stick grenades and ammunition bandolier around his neck.

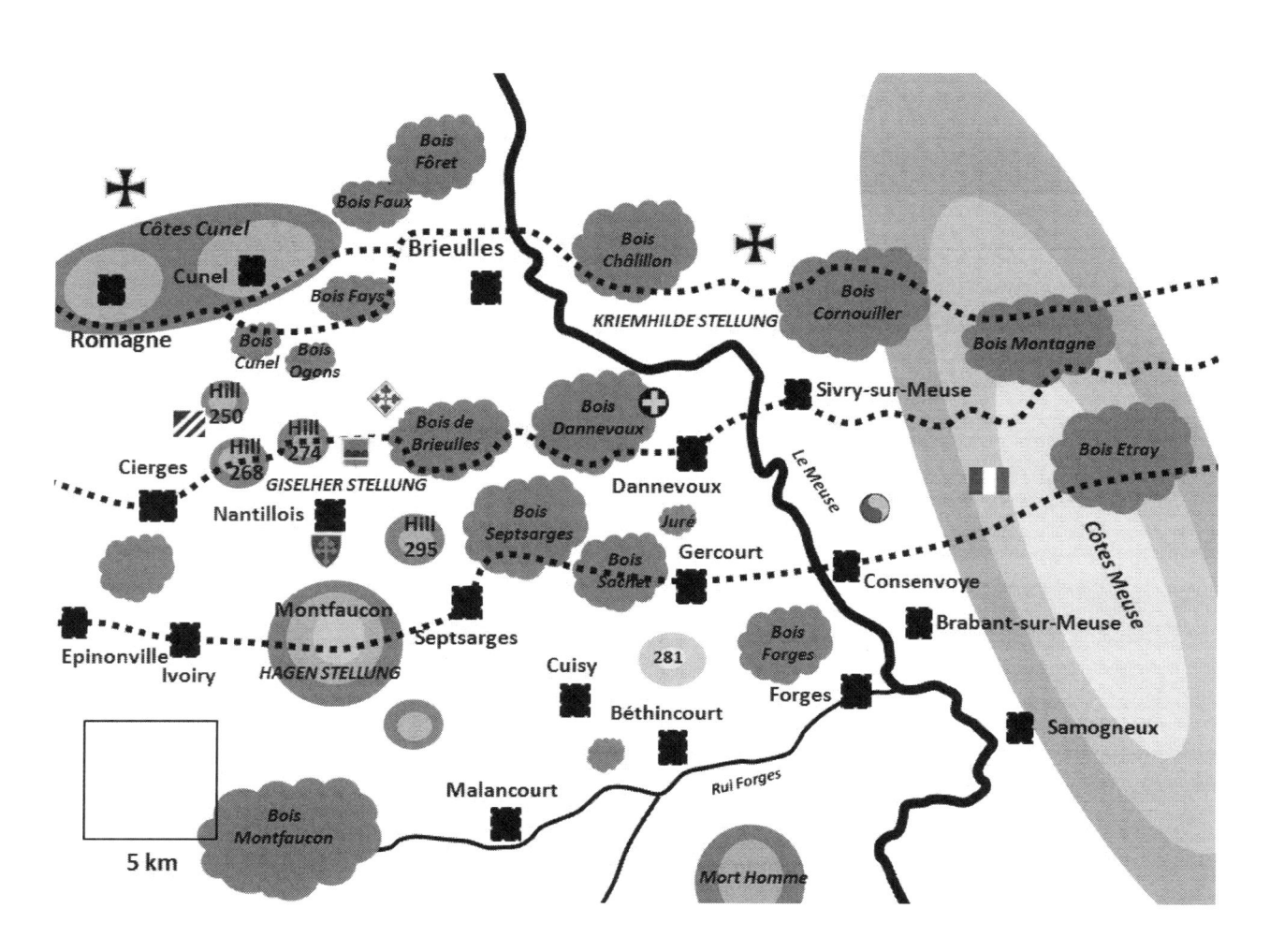

80th Division area of operations Oct. 2-3, 1918.

Overhead view of Nantillois, looking east.

80th Division During the Battle for Bois d'Ogons

Div. C.O.: Maj. Gen. Adelbert Cronkhite

C.o.S.: Col. William H. Waldron

G-1: Col. Sherburne Whipple

G-2: Maj. Cuthbert P. Noland

G-3: Col. John B. Barnes

G-4: Maj. James F. Loree

Adj.: Maj. Charles M. Jones

Surg.: Col. Thomas L Rhoads

I.G.: Maj. Albert G. Goodwyn

J.A.G.: Maj. Clifford V. Church

Ord.: Maj. Earl D. Church

French Liaison Off.: Capt. Michael Godechaux

305th Engineer Regt.: Col. George R. Spalding

305th Field Signal Bn.: Maj. E. E. Kelly

D.M.G.O.: Lt. Col. Oscar S. Foley

313th Machine Gun Bn.: Maj. Prescott Huidekopper

314th Machine Gun Bn.: Maj. Robert H. Cox

315th Machine Gun Bn.: Maj. Leland B. Garretson

305th Trains Brigade

Col. George F. Hamilton

305th Sanitary Train Bn.: Lt. Col. Elliot B. Edie

305th Motor Transport Train Bn.: Maj. J. W. O'Mahoney

155th Artillery Brigade

Brig. Gen. George G. Heiner

305th Ammunition Train Bn.: Lt. Col. Orlo C. Whitaker

305th Trench Mortar Battery: Capt. Paul B. Barringer

313th Artillery: Lt. Col. Otto L. Brunzell

1st Bn.: Maj. Francis J. Dunnigan

2nd Bn.: Capt. John Nash

314th Artillery: Col. Robert S. Welsh

1st Bn.: Maj. Howard Eager

2nd Bn.: Maj. Granville Fortescue

315th Artillery: Col. Carroll I. Goodfellow

1st Bn.: Maj. R. W. Barker

2nd Bn.: Maj. Lloyd C. Stark

3rd Bn.: Maj. Otis L. Guernsey

159th Infantry Brigade

Brig. Gen. George H. Jamerson

317th Infantry: Col. Howard R. Perry; Lt. Col. Charles Keller

1st Bn.: Maj. Powell Glass

2nd Bn.: Maj. C. C. Clifford

3rd Bn.: Maj. Walker H. Adams

318th Infantry: Col. Ulysses Grant Worrilow; Lt. Col. Chas. Mitchell
1st Bn.: Maj. Charles Sweeny
2nd Bn.: Maj. Jennings C. Wise
3rd Bn.: Maj. Henry H. Burdick

160th Infantry Brigade
Brig. Gen. Lloyd M. Brett

319th Infantry: Col. Frank S. Cocheu; Lt. Col. Gordon R. Catts
1st Bn.: Maj. Hugh H. O'Bear
2nd Bn.: Maj. James L. Montague
3rd Bn.: Capt. Gerald Egan

320th Infantry: Col. Ephraim G. Peyton; Lt. Col. William M. Gordon
1st Bn., Maj. Ashby Williams
2nd Bn., Maj. Harry P. Holt
3rd Bn., Maj. German H. H. Emory

Chapter 1

Before the Battle of Bois d'Ogons

I was drafted into the Army in August, 1917. I lived in Petersburg, Virginia, and reported right next door to Camp Lee in early September. There myself and thousands of other Selectees (as we were called) were turned into hardened American soldiers ready to beat the Government of Imperial Germany in order to help "Make the World Safe for Democracy."

I was assigned to Company B, 1st Battalion, 318th Infantry Regiment, 80th Infantry Division, Maj. Gen. Adelbert Cronkhite, commanding. I'm glad that I was. Cronkhite named us the "Blue Ridge Division" because we were built around Selectees (or draftees) from Virginia, West Virginia, and Pennsylvania. The one thing that connected them all—timelessly—were the beautiful Blue Ridge Mountains of the Appalachian Range. Although I had never seen the mountains before, I certainly did like the design. For our division motto, Cronkhite chose *Vis Monitum* or "Strength of the Mountains."

From Sept. 1917 until June 1918, the division was assembled, trained, and equipped at Camp Lee for overseas movement. In July, we crossed the great Atlantic and by August 1917, the infantry brigades (159th and 160th Infantry Brigades) of the division were training with the British in Artois and Picardy. The division's artillery brigade, the 155th Arty. Brig., trained near the coast at Redon with the French. It had two light artillery regiments that were armed with French 75mm Field Guns and one heavy artillery regiment that was armed with French 155mm Howitzers. While with Maj. Gen. Julian Byng's Third British Army near Albert, the infantry brigades participated in the Somme Offensive of 1918. This was my first action against the hated Hun. I was an Automatic Rifleman (A.R.) who fired an M1915 Chauchat. My assistant gunner (A.G.) and good friend was Earl Getz.

In Sept. 1918, infantry brigades of the division were sent south to help collapse the Saint-Mihiel Salient with General John "Black Jack" Pershing's First American Army. Because the operation was such a success, most of the division was held in reserve. My regiment, the 318th Infantry, saw no real action during this offensive.

After this, the entire 80th Division was slated for the bone-crushing and war-ending Meuse-Argonne Offensive. For this offensive, we were attached to Maj. Gen. Robert Lee Bullard's American III Corps. *Le Secteur de Meuse-Argonne* was just northwest of us, on the northwest side of Verdun, where the French famously stopped the Germans in 1915-16 ("They Shall Not Pass!"). Since then, the area had remained a hellhole—a place where neither man nor beast should have lived. Both the French and the Germans were dug in deep in this sector. It was called the Meuse-Argonne Sector because it was between the deep *Forêt d'Argonne* to the west and the great Meuse River to the east with *les Côtes de Meuse* (Heights of the Meuse) overlooking the entire area from the east. Neither side had really attacked the other since 1916 because the area was deemed impenetrable given the dominance of the terrain and the manmade defenses that complemented it. [2]

General "Black Jack" Pershing's American First Army was to advance northward between the Meuse River and the Argonne Forest, supported on its left by the French Fourth Army, which was just west of the forest. To the left of the French Fourth Army, northeast of Paris, the French were to force the Germans back from the Aisne River while farther north, French, British, and Belgian divisions, reinforced by some American divisions, were to continue the attack east toward Brussels, Liège, and Aachen.

The significance of the American First Army's northward drive up the Meuse-Argonne toward Sedan in this up-and-coming campaign lay in the fact that, if carried far enough, it would gain control of the lateral railways and divide the German Army in northern France and Belgium. If we captured Sedan, the "Hun with the Gun" would be unable to maintain his forces in France and Belgium, since communications between his two wings would be practically impossible except by the circuitous route through Liège. Furthermore, the capture or defeat of German armies west of Sedan would be practically certain because, under the powerful attacks by which the British and the Allies were currently delivering in Flanders, the Huns would not be able to conduct an orderly withdrawal through Liège.

It was evident to both sides, therefore, that it was south of Sedan that the Germans could least afford to lose ground.

And that was the very place we Americans resolved to take.

Along most of the Western Front, the Germans had prepared several defensive lines to the rear of their first position (i.e., a classic defensive-in-depth). Northwest of the Meuse-

---

[2] *Le Secteur de Meuse-Argonne* is pronounced "Lay Sec-tour day Mooze-ah Are-gone," *Forêt d'Argonne* is pronounced "Fore-et-dar-gone," and *Les Côtes de Meuse* is pronounced "Lay Coat day Mooz-ah."

Argonne Sector, the loss of ground to the Germans would have had no decisive effect as their defensive lines or belts were separated by several miles. In the Meuse-Argonne, however, where the important railways and Sedan lay comparatively close to the first line, the second and third lines were built close to the first position, forming a practically continuous defensive zone about ten miles deep. Each line had a code-name like "*HAGEN*" or "*KRIEMHILDE,*" etc.

The other factor to understand is that the Meuse-Argonne was ideal for defensive fighting. The heights just east of the Meuse constituted a formidable natural barrier and furnished splendid observation sites for the Hun. These heights and the broken hills of the sector had been organized by the Germans into almost impregnable defensive positions or *Stellung*. Between the Meuse and the Argonne Forest, for example, lay the dominating hill of *Montfaucon* (Mount Falcon), which afforded the Germans perfect observation. During the Battle of Verdun in 1916, the Crown Prince of Prussia even built a a reinforced tower atop the hill and the Germans called it "Little Gibralter."[3]

In the sector, numerous east and west running ridges lent themselves to the construction of defensive lines which connected the Heights of the Meuse, in the east, with the Argonne Forest, in the west. In organizing these lines, the Germans made extensive use of barbed-wire, trenches, concrete M.G. emplacements, and prepared artillery positions—all mutually supporting. The comparatively narrow front and the great depth of the German defenses therefore made our task an extremely difficult one. The only feasible method of breaking through such defensive strong lines (and at great cost) was to drive salients into them by launching wave after wave of frontal assaults and then roll up Germans' flanks from the salients.[4]

The defensive positions we would be facing were all on the forward crests of ridges. According to Col. Moss, these types of positions had the following strengths and weaknesses:

> *Strengths—the enemy can generally see better what is going on to their front and flanks and the men have a feeling of security that they do not enjoy on low ground, the enemy can generally reinforce the firing line better and the dead and wounded can be removed more easily, and the enemy's line of retreat is better.*

---

[3] *Stellung* is pronounced "Stel-loong" and *Montfaucon* is pronounced "Mon Fack-own."

[4] A *salient* is a wedge in the line—either in or out.

> *Weaknesses—plunging fire of a high position is not as effective as a sweeping fire of a low one and it is not as easy to conceal their position.*[5]

Of course we planned to exploit the weaknesses and talked about how we would move under their fire and through their wire.

The movement of men and *matériel* into the Meuse-Argonne was conducted with utmost secrecy, entirely under cover of darkness. Consequently, at night the overloaded roads overflowed with intermixed infantry, artillery, and service of supply (S.O.S.) units. Motor lamps, fires, or even cigarette, cigar, or pipe smoking was strickly forbidden. During the day, the roads and fields were to be clear so that German aerial scouts could not identify movement into the sector. To further mask our movement, French infantry (*Poilu*—or "Hairy Ones") remained in the forward positions.

In all, about 220,000 French soldiers were moved out of the sector and approximately 600,000 Americans were moved into it—a Herculean task. The fact that it was performed with such relative smoothness and precision, and without gaining much attention from the enemy, is a striking tribute to the ability of the American First Army and its staff. Maj. Gen. James Harbord, the commander of the S.O.S., later remembered:

> *General Pershing's immediate problem was the secret transportation over inadequate highways of approximately half-a-million men comprising fifteen full-strength divisions, most of them just out of a major engagement at St. Mihiel, and some thousands of Army troops. They had to be in place for the coming battle. Necessarily it meant night movements by marching, by rail and by trucks.... As the sector to be occupied by the American First Army was held by the French, it had to be vacated by them before the Americans could move in. Approximately 220,000 men were moved out and some 600,000 took their places, making a total of 820,000 troops handled. The work of the American Staff has received the commendation of more than one Allied authority.*[6]

To get to our concentration area just south of Meuse-Argonne, we marched during the night on muddy, dark roads—roads that most of us could not identify on a map even if our lives

---

[5] *M.M.T.* 1161.

[6] Harbord, 430.

depended on it ("Join the infantry and see the world....on foot...and in the dark!"). We would march from one wood to the next and wait out the day under cover. During the day, movement was restricted to groups of two with two hundred yards between groups, the parking of vehicles in formation was prohibited, and vehicles had to be kept either under the cover of trees or close to a building and camouflaged. Animals were also to be kept under cover, with their watering limited to groups four, and then only after 7:15 P.M. Cronkhite ordered that "Every man on the firing line or in any other part of the area must avoid being seen by the enemy. A single observation of the change in the color of the uniform will give important information."[7] Finally, about six km southwest of Verdun, near Regret, we were ordered to halt and stand by for several days in Bois La Ville, where the entire 80th Division was concentrated for the first time since we left Camp Lee.[8]

The northern edge of Bois La Ville contained a large French ammunition dump (*Dépôt Munitions*), which, together with the many French and American artillery batteries, made attractive targets for German airmen.[9] Several aerial bombing raids were in fact made while we were concentrated here, but we suffered no casualties. Aerial bombardment wasn't so bad because an aeroplane can only drop so many bombs on one's head before it had to fly off. But a battalion or brigade-sized artillery strike, that's just down-right deadly.

Bois La Ville or "Camp Gallieni" had long been a permanent rest center for French troops entering and leaving the lines around Verdun. The undergrowth in the woods had been cleared away and barracks, huts, or tents were scattered over the area. While several units occupied the camp's makeshift barracks, the bulk of the command (especially the infantry!) was quartered in tents. The men found the new area comparatively pleasant, since duties were light and they could visit friends in other units of the division. Another highlight of our brief stay at Camp Gallieni was a Y.M.C.A. show with an American woman as the feature attraction (I don't remember her name—but she was pretty). Our most-utilized diversion, however, was in reading or writing letters. One soldier from 3/320th Infantry remembered: "Most of the men wrote home every day during that short period, since each day might be the last chance in this life. Some letters were also written to be mailed only in case the writer was killed, but I don't think that there were too many of these. Because each letter home had to be censored by our platoon

---

[7] As cited in Stultz, 347.

[8] *Regret* is pronounced "Re-gret" and *Bois La Ville* is pronounced "Bwa La Veal."

[9] *En Dépôt Munitions* is pronounced "Dep-oh Mune-it-ee-own."

leader, the company's lieutenants spent most of their time reading through (and censoring) our letters. If we wrote about our location, size of our unit, troop morale, or anything that may tip the enemy off about our fighting power, it was cut right out of the letter and we received a tongue-lashing not to do it again because "letter writing is a privilege in the Army and not a right."[10]

It was here at Camp Gallieni where we received our pre-battle instructions and issues of new equipment, including repeating shotguns that we generally called "trench brooms." The most common model was the Model 12 Winchester, an upgrade of the M1897 that was used in the Philippines to combat insurgents. The M12 is a .12 gauge weapon that uses a pump action in combination with an attached tubular magazine (under the barrel) that can spray loads of .32 cal. pellets over an area with deadly speed.

"Sha-Clack."

"Boom!"

"Sha-Clack."

"Boom!"

"Sha-Clack."

"Boom!"

Some of the trench brooms were even fitted to take a M1917 Enfield Bayonets, and together, we called them "combat trombones." The only drawback to the weapon, aside for its close range, was that its shell casings were made from cardboard and cardboard sucks up moisture really fast. Other equipment was given a last inspection, gas masks were again tested, and large quantities of grenades of various types were issued and demonstrated (e.g., the M2 "Pineapple Grenade"). With all of this equipment, our infantry platoons packed more of a combat punch than that of our enemy.

Pyrotechnics with a code for their use were distributed to company commanders and platoon leaders and were demonstrated by French officers. These pyrotechnics included day and

---
[10] As cited in Stultz, 349-50.

night rockets and flares (e.g., *Véry* Lights). Battle maps were issued to all officers, with known German positions and the pre-planned artillery barrage lines noted. Letters, diaries and other identification were ordered destroyed before entering the front lines.

We all knew that the 1916 battle of Verdun was one of the biggest and bloodiest battles of the war thus far. It was when the German General-in-Chief at the time, *Generalfeldmarschal* Erich von Falkenhayn, ordered the Prussian Crown Prince Wilhelm's German Fifth Army to attack the strong French defenses of the *Région Fortifiée Verdun* (R.F.V.) and those of the French Second Army on the right bank of the Meuse. Falkenhayn intended to capture *les Côtes de Meuse* from which Verdun could be overlooked and bombarded with observed artillery fire.[11] Once taken, the French would no doubt be *provoked* into trying to retake the decisive heights and as the did so, they would be smashed and bled white by superior German fire power.

On February 21, 1916, Falkenhayn's great offensive (code-named *Unternehmen Gericht* or "Operation Judgment") against Verdun began and in fact drove the French back upon *Côtes Meuse*.[12] By March 6, 1916, some twenty French divisions were committed to the defense of Verdun, which defended an ancient crossing of the Meuse. *Général de France* Philippe Pétain ordered that no withdrawals were to be made and that counter-attacks were to be conducted, despite exposing French infantry to German massed artillery. To better communicate this directive, *Général de France* Robert Nivelle, one of Pétain's loyal lieutenants, coined the phrase: "*Ils ne passeront pas!*" or "They Shall Not Pass!"[13]

The road from Bar-de-Luc in the south to Verdun in the north was called *le Voie Sacrèe* ("The Sacred Way") and it kept the French soldiers there supplied with food, water, and ammunition.[14]

By April, French artillery on the west bank of the Meuse finally reached parity with the Germans, and the French started to inflict thousands of casualties on the Hun atop the Heights of the Meuse.

---

[11] *Generalfeldmarschal* Erich von Falkenhayn is pronounced "Gen-er-awl Feld-marshall Er-eek von Falk-en-highn" and *Région Fortifiée Verdun* is pronounced "Rage-on Fort-ee-fay Ver-done."

[12] *Unternehmen Gericht* is pronounced "Oon-ter Nay-men Ger-rickt."

[13] *Général de France Robert Nivelle* is pronounced "Gin-air-awl day Frawnce Row-bear Row-bear Nee-veal" and *Ils ne passeront pas* is pronounced "Eel nee Pass-or-awn Pa."

[14] *Le Voie Sacrèe* is pronounced "Lay Vwa Sack-ray."

To change the dynamic, Falkenhayn shifted his attacks into the Meuse-Argonne Sector, which was on the west bank of the Meuse in order to flank Verdun from the north. French reinforcements contained the attacks, however, especially atop a steep elevation, which came to be called *Côtes de Mort Homme* ("Dead Men Hill") that is just southeast of Béthincourt.[15] To support the French at Verdun, the British launched a massive (and failed) offensive up the Somme River in July (Somme Offensive, 1916) and it became one of the most bloody offensives of the war (the British Army was never the same after the Somme). Although the British failed to break through all of the Germans' defensive lines in the Somme, they were able to draw enough German forces away from Verdun to enable the French to stabilize the line there. We were told that both sides lost around 500,000 at the Battle of Verdun, an average of about 80,000 casualties for each month of the battle. Ever since then, the fighting in the area had been desultory at best, because it was one of the most difficult to take—for both sides. According to Maj. Gen. Robert Lee Bullard, who commanded the American III Corps in the Meuse-Argonne:

> *To what nature had, perhaps without design, created in the way of defenses, military art had contributed every device known to modern war. Old, rusty, new, twisted, straight, netted, crossed and overlapping barbed wire was getting strung in endless miles with fortified strong points, dugouts, concrete M.G. emplacements, skillfully selected natural M.G. sites, and many lines of trenches flanking and in parallel depth. It was probably the most comprehensive system of leisurely prepared field defenses known to history.*[16]

All told, the 80th Division spent five days in Bois La Ville hiding out by day and training by night. One soldier from 3/320th Infantry remembered:

> *We knew that we were on the verge of a big drive, and had frequent conferences, at which, thanks to the wisdom of the major, the sergeants who commanded the platoons, as well as the officers, were present. Our stay at here is chiefly remembered by the men for one evening when the whole regiment was led on a sort of "follow the leader" stunt through the woods. The object was to see if we could keep "closed-up" and avoid splitting up and losing part of the outfit, and it was a thorough enough test, for we had double-timed through the*

---

[15] *Côtes de Mort Homme* is pronounced "Lay Coat day More Oam" and *Béthincourt* is pronounced "Beth-awn-core."

[16] As cited in Bullard, 433.

woods, jumped logs and turned sharp corners aplenty before we finally regained the main road and reorganized the column.[17]

Also during this time, many reconnaissance missions were conducted by our officers to the jump-off lines, which were currently thinly held by units of the French Army and the American 33rd (Prairie) Division. As was already stated, America's Blue Ridge Division was transferred to Maj. Gen. Robert Lee Bullard's American III Corps, which was to be centered around Mort Homme. It was to be used as part of the supporting effort to break through the strong German lines in the vicinity of Montfaucon.

Bullard was a Pershing favorite. He was a tall, athletic, 57-year-old Regular Army officer from Alabama who had commanded the American 1st Division at Cantigny. He had drive, and in our opinion, a ruthless disregard for losses.

But how else was he supposed to feel?

The day before the big attack began, for example, Bullard sternly instructed his division commanders (like our very own Cronkhite) not to worry about their flanks. "In every previous fight," he told them, "I heard division, brigade, and regimental commanders excuse their failures to continue the advance by blaming the units on their right or left for failing to come forward with them." In this battle, he would "take no such excuse... each of your divisions maintains its reserve for the very purpose of protecting its flanks."

There would be no excuses—this time, they would attack, whatever the cost.

And we ground pounders were the cost.

As far as "forget about the flanks" goes, Bullard was right. We found that each brigade, battalion, company, or platoon should in fact advance as far as it could without worrying about the unit to their left or right.

Should each unit defend its own flanks? Absolutely! But the message was to stick as many knives into the German hog as possible, creating salients in their lines—making them react to us and not us reacting to them.

---

[17] As cited in Stultz, 347-48.

So each corps, division, brigade, etc., was to advance to their assigned objectives without waiting for their flanks to be secure. This meant that we had to maintain 360° security at all times, especially in the woods, in order to prevent getting hit in flank or rear.

The advance to the American First Army's initial objective, *Côtes de Cunel*, however, was to be paced by Cameron's V Corps, which was in the center of the Army axis of advance with the 79th Infantry Division. *HAGEN, GISELHER* and *KRIEMHILDE* were expected to be breached on the first day (!), and *FREYA* the next. As we shall see, many days and nights—and weeks—were to pass before this goal was attained.[18]

The fact that Pershing or Foch even expected us to breach one of these lines in one day was either cruel, arrogant, or sly. Pershing would often say to his corps and division commanders during the offensive: "You're behind schedule! You're behind schedule!" It's like saying that I should be able to drive from Richmond to San Fransisco in one hour. Every hour above that, I'd be late.

It's a ridiculous assumption—but a motivator.

The first unit of America's Blue Ridge Division to move north from Bois la Ville to the front line was 3/319th Infantry. It marched during the night of Sept. 21-22 to *Bois Bourrus*, where it relieved 3/131st Infantry, 33rd (Prairie) Division, which held a reserve position in the Béthincourt sector. The Prairie Division had occupied the support line with only a thin line of French troops remaining in the forward positions south of *Ruisseau Forges* (Forges Creek) to screen the relief.[19]

The 80th Division's mission was to punch through the German outpost line at Béthincourt (code-named "Wiesenschlecken"), breach the first line, *HAGEN*, at Gercourt, and advance up to *Village Dannevoux*, which was about eight km north of Forges Creek, was the corps' designated Line of Departure (L.D.).[20] From there, we were to break through the

---

[18] *Côtes de Cunel* is pronounced "Coat day Que-nel." According to Germanic legend, *Hagen* was the German Burgundian knight who killed his supposed friend Siegfried by stabbing him in the back, *Giselher* was the King of Burgundy who Siegfried helped to marry *Brünhilde* (Siegfried had to climb a mountain, go through a ring of fire, and awaken *Brünhilde* from a spell with a kiss, i.e., "Sleeping Beauty"), *Kriemhilde* was Siegfried's wife and *Giselher's* sister and *Freya* was *Wotan's* wife (*Wotan* is King of the Gods) and *Freya* is the Goddess of Love, Sexuality, Beauty, Fertility, Gold, etc.

[19] *Bois Bourrus* is pronounced "Bwa Borrows" and *Ruisseau Forges* is pronounced "Reese-sew Forge."

[20] *Gercourt* is pronounced "Geyr-core" and *Village Dannevoux* is pronounced "Veal-awg Dan-ev-voo."

GISELHER, KRIEMHILDE, and *FREYA* (*KRIEMHILDE* being the strongest along Côtes de Cunel) in conjunction with other American First Army units and continue the advance "in the open" toward Sedan until the Germans surrendered. The division sector was be about two km wide (each attack battalion covering one km and each attack company 500 meters), or about one km on each side of the ruins of Béthincourt south of *Rui Forges*.[21]

As per Army doctrine, Cronkhite directed the Blue Ridge Division to attack in column of brigades, the 160th Brigade leading. The Infantry regiments were to be side-by-side in column of battalions—Col. Frank Cocheu's 319th Infantry on the right and Lt. Col. Ephraim G. Peyton's 320th Infantry on the left. Each regiment would then attack in column of battalions: assault, support, and reserve. Each company would then attack with two platoons up and two in back. The support battalion would "mop-up" postions by-passed by the assault battalion and protect the regiment's flanks while the reserve battalion provided ammunition and supply details for the assault battalion. Once the assault battalion shot its bolt, it would be replaced by the support battalion, etc. And once the attacking brigade was beaten into pulp, the other brigade would come up behind it and repeat the process.

We all knew that the only way to break these strong defensive lines would be to "attack in depth" and the way the A.E.F. divisions were purposely organized, depth would be achieved.

The advance was to proceed at a rate of one hundred meters every four minutes through the enemy outpost line about a km north of Béthincourt, then through *HAGEN* at Gercourt, and up to Côtes Dannevoux and *GISELHER*. It was important for the infantry to get from "Point A to B" at exact times in order to maintain artillery support, which was rigidly pre-planned. Cronkhite's battle orders stated, in part:

> *It is directed that the attack be pushed with vigor and that each leading battalion continue the advance until slowed down, when it will be passed by the next battalion in rear as directed by the brigade commander. It is not intended to use more than one brigade to [breach HAGEN und GISELHER]. When the objective has been attained, the troops occupying it will at once reform and take up the organization of the ground for defense in depth and the police of the battlefield.*[22]

---

[21] *Rui Forges* is short for Forges Creek. It is pronounced "Roo Four-jez."

[22] As cited in Stultz, 365.

To make a long story short, from Sept. 26-30, the 80th Division broke through *HAGEN* at Gercourt and *GISELHER* at Dannevoux. But not all was well for the rest of the American First Army, as the Germans were holding tough along *KRIEMHILDE*—the strongest of their lines—in the vicinity of Cunel. The Allied commander-in-chief, Ferdinand Foch, was in fact so alarmed that he considered calling off the attack in the Meuse-Argonne, especially considering the great advances the British were making in Flanders. But Pershing assured Foch that his Doughboys would in fact break through *FREYA,* drive north up the Meuse River Valley, and take Sedan from the south, even if it meant the death of every one of us. The conversation was relayed to us by "Joe Latrinsky" in this way:

"But we cannot afford such losses, *mon ami*," Foch reportedly said to Pershing.

"You're right general, and I don't intend to take any more than I need to. But rest assured, the American Army will take Sedan!"

"Well general , if you need any more support, you will let me know, no?"

"Yes sir. I need the French corps on my flanks to push farther and faster. The guns on the Heights of the Meuse are tearing my men to pieces!"

"*Oui, général*, we must get them moving."[23]

"Thank you, sir." With that, Pershing returned to his H.Q. to meet with his corps commanders Bullard, Liggett, and Cameron, "Gentlemen," he said, according to Joe Latrinsky who used a Mark Twain accent as Pershing was from Missouri, "I am under extreme pressure to keep the attack moving forward. The British are driving the Germans back at Arras and we have an opportunity to snag hundreds of thousands of the enemy if we take Sedan within the next few days. I know the men are tired, I know we have a lot of inexperienced officers. Corps commanders, I need you to lay the wood. Replace anyone you want. There are no bad soldiers, only bad officers. Be relentless. Get up to the front and put fire into these people and make them realize that we have a chance to end the war right now, in just a few weeks. If we don't, the Germans will simply pull back in an orderly fashion, reestablish their lines, and this war may last until 1920. Do you understand?"

---

[23] "Joe Latrinsky" was a fictitious soldier who spread the "rumor mill." When we prefaced our remark with, "According to Joe," we knew it was a rumor.

"Yes, sir," they answered in a choral response. And of course Bullard had to pitch in (using a thick Mississippi accent that bothered even we Tidewater, Virginia-types): "Sir, we will break through even if it takes every single one of my men, including me and my staff."

"That's what I want to hear, Bull, now get moving!"

Clearly none of us were there during this exchange, but "Joe" was and that was our understanding of the "low-down." Writing after the war, Lt. Lukens of the 320th Infantry noted pretty much what we all were thinking while we were the Meuse-Argonne:

> *Things were not moving as rapidly up front as they had at the first jump-off. As our own first drive had shown us, the thick woods which checkerboard the hills [of the sector], and which had not been fought over since the Huns originally took them, made far-more difficult going than the bald, shell-pocked hills around Verdun. The nature of the country lent itself wonderfully to the defensive plans of the Boche; the proportion of forest to clearing was just about enough so that all the clearings were covered by the field of fire from unseen guns in the woods, while the woods were filled with snipers and accurately ranged for artillery. The job was done by brute force, a division going in on a narrow sector and advancing in spite of everything until its momentum was lost, then another one relieving it and doing the same thing.*[24]

For the rest of the day of Oct. 1, the infantry regiments of the 80th Division either maintained their positions or continued to move into their new positions while batteries from Heiner's 155th Arty. Brig. provided fire support for the Prairie Division in the vicinity of Dannevoux. In so doing, Heiner's artillery suffered a few casualties and five soldiers from the 314th Artillery were cited for exceptional gallantry during the day's operations: 1Sgt. Harold Marshall of Battery A, Sergeant Charles R. Shelton of Battery A, Private Glenn D. Hughes of Battery A, Private Roy E. Burroughs of Battery B, and Private Walter L. Paynes of Battery B:

> *On Oct. 1, 1918, 1Sgt. Marshal was in charge of a detail to load and unload ammunition. The ammunition trucks to which this detail was assigned became jammed on Cuisy Ridge. The road on which the truck was halted was under heavy enemy shell fire. Sergeant Marshall, by his own coolness and courage,*

---

[24] As cited in *3/320th Infantry*, 77-78.

succeeded in extricating the trucks from the jam and bringing the ammunition safely to the battery positions.

On Oct. 1, 1918, Sergeant Shelton was in charge of a detail of men from A/314 at the ammunition dump near Cuisy. Although the dump was subjected to heavy shell fire Sgt. Shelton continued to move ammunition from the dump until all of the ammunition had been removed to safety.

On Oct. 1, 1918, Private Hughes was acting as a telephone operator at the battalion O.P. on Dannevoux Ridge. Pvt. Hughes was wounded by a shell fragment while at his post but he nevertheless continued to operate the telephone and refused to leave until ordered to do so by his battery commander.

On the afternoon of Oct. 1, 1918, on Hill 262, the Number 1 Gun of B/314 received a direct hit from a German shell, most of the gun crew either being killed or wounded. Pvt. Burroughs carried to safety three members of this gun crew. This work was done under continued heavy shelling of the battery positions.

For us in 1/318th Infantry, Oct. 1 was spent clawing our way further north through Bois Brieulles between *GISELHER* and *KRIEMHILDE* with units from the 4th (Ivy) Division. Although we suffered some casualties, it was actually a pretty light day, considering that it was between two of the Germans' main defensive lines. Our patrols reported some enemy activity beyond *GISELHER* but we all knew, "for certain sure," that the ridge to our front, on which *Village Cunel* and *KRIEMHILDE* was located, was infested with Hun, thick as fleas on a mangy dog from Norfolk. And in front of it was a huge open field with outstanding fields of fire. In fact, the Hun were probably licking their chops waiting for us to attack.

Get out the shovels boys!

It was the waiting for the inevitable that I think was the worst part.

To the south, in Bois Montfaucon with Brett's 160th Inf. Brig., their recovery operations were going as well as expected, although the men were still paying the price for the decision to leave the majority of their packs behind. Lt. Lukens of I/3/320th Infantry remembered:

We went on back, knowing that our job was done for the time being, stopping when chance offered to pick up a loaf of bread or a can of tomatoes from a pile of rations, or to fill our stomachs and canteens at a spring, or to "bum" a smoke, and in this way we drifted back until we came upon our kitchens, where we found a meal of hot canned beef and coffee waiting, our first real honest meal since four days or more... The comforts of our new position were not expensive, as half of our blankets had been lost, and there was no further weather protection for the men than the "bivvies" they could construct.[25]

Due to his superior leadership, Col. James Cocheu, commander of the 319th Infantry, was tapped for promotion and sent to the General Staff School in Langres to eventually serve as the Operations Officer for the III Corps. He was replaced by Col. James Love, the 318th Infantry's one-time X.O. Maj. Hugh O'Bear, the commander of 1/319, was also tapped for promotion and was also transferred out of the division. All other major leadership positions stayed in place, until our second drive, which would take a real toll on the Blue Ridge Division.[26]

October 2, 1918.

Weather: Rain.

Roads: Heavy.

On Oct. 2, as Pershing and his corps commanders adjusted their lines to punch through *KRIEMHILDE*—the main German defensive line—General Cronkhite was ordered to concentrate the entire 80th Division just south of *Bois des Ogons* (or *Bois d'Ogons*), between Hill 274 and Bois Brieulles, with Jamerson's 159th Inf. Brig. designated as the attack brigade and Brett's 160th Inf. Brig. as the reserve brigade. The object would be to breach *KRIEMHILDE* in the vicinity of *Village Cunel*. While two battalions of the 318th Infantry would be arrayed to lead

---

[25] As cited in *3/320th Infantry*, 75.

[26] *319th Infantry*, 29.

the attack into Bois d'Ogons, my battalion, 1/318, was to remain in Bois Brieulles until relieved by a unit from the Ivy Division.[27]

This was to be the big fat fight for the 80th Division, our *sine qua non*.[28]

For the up-and-coming fight, it was decided to breach KRIEMHILDE with Col. Woorilow's 318th Infantry (-) on the left, adjoining with elements of the 3rd (Rock of the Marne) Division near Hill 268 and and Col. Howard R. Perry's 317th Infantry on the right, adjoining with with 1/318 in Bois Brieulles.[29] Brett's 160th Inf. Brig., the reserve brigade, would be concentrated near Septsarges, and Heiner's 155th Arty. Brig., currently providing artillery support for the Prairie Division, would be brought over to support the infantry brigades of the 80th Division south of Nantillois.

With receipt of the order to deploy south of Nantillois, Welsh, as the artillery brigade operations officer, sent his battalion and battery commanders, and his scouts and markers out to the area between Septsarges and Nantillois to conduct an R.S.O.P. While conducting said reconnaissance, Capt. Shelton Piney of 1/313th Artillery was wounded in the foot and Capt. Penniman took command of the battalion with Lt. Morgan taking command of C/1/313th Artillery. With the R.S.O.P. complete, it was decided to place the 314th Artillery between Septsarges and Hill 295. While C/1/314th Artillery would be the accompanying battery for Worrilow's 318th Infantry (-), a battery from the 313th Artillery was assigned to be the accompanying battery for the 317th Infantry.[30]

In preparation for the new offensive, Brett's 160th Inf. Brig. moved northeast from Bois Montfaucon and took up positions around Cuisy. Maj. Ashby Williams of 1/320th remembered:

As we were going down the hill into Cuisy. I remember a Boche plane came over. flying very low and firing his A.R. as he came. My men opened fire on him but he got away, apparently unhurt. He was evidently looking for the French artillery which was camouflaged along the road and I remember how the French gunners beat a hasty retreat to their cover to prevent having their

---

[27] *Bois d'Ogons* is pronounced "Bwa Doe-gawn."

[28] *Sine qua non* is Lation for "reason of existence."

[29] *Nantillois* is pronounced "Nawn-till-lou-wah."

[30] *314th Artillery*, 39; *317th Infantry*, 63.

pictures taken. We then proceeded down through the town of Cuisy and up the ridge to the south of it. Here the brigade adjutant came up and said that it was the general's plan that the brigade should occupy the trench systems along the parallel ridges, one in front of Cuisy, one in back of it, and the other in back of that, the 320th on the right and the 319th on the left. I hastily drew up a plan in accordance with this direction and sent it to the other battalions of this regiment and the other regiment. Ultimately, however, the ridge in front of Cuisy was under such constant and heavy shell fire that the battalions located there had to move back to the ridge back of Cuisy... From the ridge where my troops were located the country round about spread out in panoramic view. Indeed, the terrain thereabout presented some aspects of unusual interest, both from tactical and historical points of view. To the northwest, about a mile-and-a-half distant, standing in its majestic desolation on a bold summit, was the historic town of Montfaucon, which had been such a formidable stumbling block in the way of the 79th Division a few days before. It was from a high tower in this town that the German Crown Prince is said to have watched, with the aid of powerful glasses, the great battle of Verdun. A few miles to the southeast was Bethincourt and the famous Dead Man's Hill, where we had jumped off a few days before in the sector to our right. Just in front of us in the valley, not more than a few hundred yards away, were the walls of the little town of Cuisy, battered to pieces by the German guns searching for the French artillery that lined the slope just beyond the town. Indeed, the Germans never ceased to shell the town and the area thereabout while we were there... The terrain around Cuisy, and as far as the eye could see for that matter, was a series of parallel ridges absolutely devoid of trees or habitations of man. The whole country presented the aspect of having been especially fashioned by some devilish hand for the special purpose of fighting man against man, and the appearance was heightened by the fact that every ridge was furrowed and seamed on its crest and forward slope by a network of trenches and the valleys and slopes were massed with wire entanglements that had been battered to pieces in the fighting that had taken place a few days before. Indeed, one was impelled to admire the splendid valor of the troops of the 4th Division who took the area. The toll of dead and wounded must have been terrific, although there was no way we could tell, because the battlefield had been policed up before we reached the place.[31]

As we in the 159th Inf. Brig. waited for the final attack order, we were subjected to relentless artillery and gas attacks throughout the day and during the night. According to Lt. Craighill of 2/317th Infantry: "Gas sentries necessarily had to be on all night, and several times the alarm was given and our needed rest disturbed."[32] Lingering gas was always a problem, and arsenic poisoning of water in the bottom of shell holes was known to occur. Mustard gas, which could eat flesh like lye, particularly in damp and moist areas like the Meuse-Argonne, would often destroy the testicles of those who took shelter in the craters where the gas lingered. I would also like to note that a mustard gas injury often had long-term effects. Some Doughs returned home disfigured from it. For example, during the 1920s, several American municipalities possessed the temerity to make it illegal for a disfigured veteran to even walk down a public street without wearing a mask. The law was called "Being Ugly in Public." Can you believe that!?

Rocked and blasted for almost a week straight, some of us began to crack (myself included), but the higher-ups refused to change their plans. No matter what, they insisted, the Blue Ridge Boys would breach *KRIEMHILDE* even if it meant the death of every last one of us (don't worry, as there was another division somewhere out there to replace us). As for me, I thought that my life was worth more, but if Germany had won the war, retaining Belgium and Luxemburg, much of the East like most of present-day Poland, Ukraine, and the Baltic States, and gaining several Belgian and French colonies, then Great Britain would probably be next. And after them, would no doubt come us. Besides, if Britain and France lost, they'd no doubt renege on repaying their war loans to U.S. banks, collapsing our already-fragile economy. That was what Joe Latrinsky told us, anyway.

Some readers may wonder why I have foot-noted other authors when discussing division operations. The answer is easy. During the war, I only really understood what was going on in my squad or platoon—sometimes company. In the Army, one is little interested with what does not directly concern him, and while I found after the war that we all had similar experiences, I do not want to deliver a "Joe Latrinsky" to the reader. Again, what we remember, we write, and

---

[31] As cited in *1/320th Infantry*, 89-90.

[32] *317th Infantry*, 61.

what we don't or won't, we don't. Much of this, for us lowly Doughs at least, is at best a fuzzy memory, clouded by the trauma of war.

As the men of America's Blue Ridge Division awaited the up-and-coming assault against *KRIEMHILDE*, we were occasionally awed/entertained/horrified by what went on above us, in the air. Every day, sometimes twice a day, we'd get raided by Hun aircraft flying in from the north. My platoon called them "J.E.B. Stuart's" after the famous Confederate cavalry Maj. Gen. "Jeb" Stuart from Virginia who was known for his lightning raids during our failed War for Southern Independence. Maj. Ashby Williams of 1/320th Infantry, in his trench near Cuisy, remembered one particular air battle that occurred above him:

> *[My particular area] was lined with six-inch howitzers that never ceased to fire day and night. The fire of these guns was observed and directed by an observer in a balloon suspended high in the air to the right of the guns. The Boche planes were constantly trying to destroy the balloon and thus put out the eyes of the big guns. His first two trials were a failure, although the shots were well-enough directed to compel the observer to take to his parachute and jump to the ground, a distance of perhaps two hundred meters. The third time the Boche came after the balloon, the plane dived out of a cloud that hung rather low that day and heading with his nose straight to the balloon, fired with his M.G., using incendiary bullets, the blue traces of which could be plainly seen going into the gas bag of the balloon. The observer jumped with his parachute and the balloon had gone up in smoke before he reached the ground. It was a beautiful and a thrilling sight. It was a drama and a tragedy in real life with 10,000 spectators looking on. Of course our M.G.s and our riflemen, too, for that matter, opened fire on the Boche plane, sending thousands of shots in his direction, but he got away apparently unharmed and no doubt rejoicing at his quarry. I admired that Boche extravagantly and so did many others who saw that heroic act, and I believe that if he had fallen into our hands we would have treated him as a real hero. Such is the sporting instinct of an American soldier.*[33]

---

[33] As cited in *1/320th Infantry*, 91.

October 3, 1918.

Weather: Fair.

Roads: Heavy.

"The morning of Oct. 3 burst forth beautifully clear with a faint mist hanging in the valleys," remembered Lt. Craighill of the 317th Infantry. "But for the occasional burst of a shell you would hardly believe that a war was in progress."[34] I remember waking up that morning wrapped in our dirty shelter half while Getz manned the "Sho-sho." I remember being tired, cold, stiff, and hungry. In fact, that's what I remember the most from the war—the feeling of total discomfort marked by extreme periods of fear, hate, and action. Getz probably said to me when I woke up:

"Good morning sunshine! Did you have a good night's rest!?"

"Uh, no."

"Well there there, now, what can Papa Getz do to make you feel better?"

"How about a cold glass of beer, a warm bed, and a hot woman?"

"No can do, brother, because I already got 'em! You missed it all while you were sleeping!"

"I'll bet that they were as ugly as you!"

"Maybe so, but beggars can't be choosy. How about some Corn Willy and coffee?"

"How about a steak?"

"Sure, as long as it looks like Corn Willy!"

At 8:00 A.M., orders were received from division, whose P.C. was in a ravine between Béthincourt and Cuisy, along the Béthincourt-Cuisy Road. Exerpts from the order are as follows:

---

[34] *317th Infantry*, 61.

80th Infantry Division.

A.E.F.

F.O. 17

Oct. 3, 1918

MAP: DUN SUR MEUSE: 1/20,000

3. 159th Infantry Brigade
(a) the 159th Brigade will lead the attack in the 80th Div. Zone.
(b) The initial disposition for the attack will be with Regiments side by side, the 317th on the right, the 318th Inf. (less 1 bn.) on the left; each regiment in column of battalions. The rear battalion, 317th Inf. will constitute the Brigade reserve at the disposal of the Brigade Commander.
(c) The zone of action and objectives as indicated on maps furnished.
(d) One Co. 313th M. G. Bn. is assigned to the 317th Inf. and one Co. to the 318th Inf. They will report at the time and places to be designated by the regimental commanders.
(e) During the night of D-1 day units will occupy positions as indicated verbally by the Brigade Commander. All units will be in position by 4:30 a.m. on D day....
(g) One Btry., 313th F. A., will be placed at the disposal of each regiment of Infantry, as accompanying artillery. One Btry. will be held at the disposal of the Brigade Commander. Batteries assigned to regiments of infantry will report at the time and places to be designated by regimental commanders.
(h) Brigade Reserve consisting of 1 bn., 317th Inf., 2 Cos. 313th M. G. Bn., 1 Btry. 313th F. A., and 1 Co. 305th Regt. of Engrs., will occupy the following positions: Bn. 317th Inf. 500 M. east of Fayel Fme. ravine N. of Montfaucon-Cuisy road; M. G. Cos., vicinity of Trench des Fainaentes 1 km. E. of Montfaucon; Art. Btry. point to be designated later; Co. Engrs. in Trench running E. from Malancourt-Montfaucon road 200 Ms. S. of and parallel to Montfaucon-Cuisy road.

By order of the Commander.
WALDRON, Chief of Staff.

Field Order 17 called for the battalions of the 159th Inf. Brig., minus 1/318, which remained in its forward position in Bois Brieulles, to assemble between Nantillois and Bois Brieulles. At 1:30 P.M., General Jamerson, the commander of the 159th Inf. Brig., met with all of his regimental and battalion commanders in blown-up Nantillois. He delivered a verbal order that outlined the army's plan of attack for the next day, Oct. 4, 1918. The commanders were told that the decimated 79th (Cross of Lorraine) Division had been replaced by the veteran 3rd (Rock of the Marne) Division, recently-arrived from Saint-Mihiel, and that Jamerson's 159th Inf. Brig. would lead the attack in the 80th Division's zone by maneuvering north up the right side of the Nantillois-Cunel Road, blow past Hill 274, attack through Bois d'Ogons and Ferme Madeleine, and storm *KRIEMHILDE* at Cunel (the objective).[35] In the bigger picture, the 3rd Division was to attack Cunel from the west, the 4th Division was to attack it from the east, and the 80th (Blue Ridge) Division was to attack it "hey diddle, diddle, right up the middle" (i.e., a double-envelopment with the 80th Division holding the middle).

Enveloping Attack

Cover the front of the enemy with sufficient force to hold his attention and, with the rest of your command, strike a flank more or less obliquely. Since your line is now longer than his, and you have more rifles in action, your fire is converging while that of your enemy's is diverging. Never attempt the envelopment of both flanks unless you greatly outnumber your enemy. Cooperation between the frontal and enveloping attack is essential to success. The fraction of the command that envelops the enemy is generally larger than that part in his front. A wide turning movement is not an enveloping movement. It is dangerous because your troops are separated and can be defeated in detail. In an enveloping movement your line will usually be continuous; it simply overlaps and envelops the enemy. An enveloping attack will nearly always result locally in a frontal attack, for it will meet the enemy's reserve. Let us repeat: do not attempt a wide turning movement. Your forces will be separated, they may not be able to assist each other, and can be defeated in detail. The

---

[35] *Ferme Madeleine* or "Farm Madeleine" is pronounced "Fairm-ah Mad-awl-ayn."

tendency of a beginner is to attempt a wide turning movement. The error of dispersion is then committed.[36]

As stated in the above directive, "never attempt the envelopment of both flanks unless you greatly outnumber your enemy. Cooperation between the frontal and enveloping attack is essential to success. The fraction of the command that envelops the enemy is generally larger than that part in his front." It was essential, then, that the flanks of the attack, i.e., the 3rd and 4th Divisions, be "larger that that part in front," which was us. Once our officers learned of the plan, they started to quote, by memory, Alfred Lord Tennyson's famous stanza from "The Charge of the Light Brigade":

"Forward, the Light Brigade! Charge for the guns!" he said:

Into the Valley of Death rode the 600.

"Forward, the Light Brigade!"

Was there a man dismay'd?

Not tho' the soldier knew

Someone had blunder'd:

Theirs not to make reply,

Theirs not to reason why,

Theirs but to do and die.

Up to this point, from Sept. 26-Oct. 3, America's Blue Ridge Division had captured 35 Hun officers, 815 men, 21 pieces of artillery, 23 trench mortars, 92 M.G.s, lots of ammunition and stores, including over five million rounds of small arms ammunition, and over 5,000 boxes of hand grenades. The German stores at Dannevoux alone valued at more than $10 million. In our first major action, Brett's 160th Inf. Brig. had attacked along a two km front which widened to five, had advanced nine km and reached its assigned objective (*GISELHER*) by midnight of the first day of the battle.

The only other division to reach the Army objective during the First Push was the 33rd (Prairie) Division, which was to our right. To be fair, the Prairie Division in fact had a couple km

---

[36] *P.M.*, 243-44.

less distance to travel than we did in the 80th Division and the German Second Position (*GISELHER*) did not extend across its sector, like it did in ours, it had only one woods to conquer instead of a half-dozen, and it had no strongly held heights barring its way. But they certainly did suffer lots of casualties from artillery that was fired from the Heights of the Meuse!

The truth is that German tenacity increased generally in proportion to the distance west of the Meuse. For example, the Prairie Division suffered 296 casualties on Sept. 26 and its total for Sept. 26-Oct. 7 was 1,370, with 197 K.I.A., including one regiment's loss of 588 wounded to 53 dead. During this period the Prairie Division put all four of its infantry regiments into line along the river when it took over the 80th Division's front as well as its own. Since it staged no attacks after Sept. 26 until Oct. 8, its casualty list demonstrates the effectiveness of German artillery firing from the Heights of the Meuse.

In contrast, the Blue Ridge Division's casualties from Sept. 26-Oct. 3 were 1,100, with 252 K.I.A. This figure includes the 150 casualties suffered by the 318th Infantry while with the 4th Division. Of the 252 K.I.A., 166 were from infantry regiments (66%). In comparison, the 4th Division suffered 2,627 casualties, with 564 K.I.A. in its infantry regiments. The 79th (Cross of Lorraine) Division, which was assigned the horrible job of attacking Montfaucon frontally, suffered a whopping 3,529 casualties, including 740 K.I.A. in its infantry regiments.

Several factors kept the 80th Division's casualties relatively low. We believe that the most important was that in Cronkhite there was no desire to make any personal "reputation" at a needless cost in life. He had nothing more to prove to the Army, as he had already "been there/done that." Was he resolute that the subordinate units of the division took the assigned objectives? Yes. But not to merely enhance his prestige within the Army bureaucracy. Cronkhite simply wanted it taken on time. Another advantage that we had is that most of our field grade officers were solid performers and we were generally spared from bungling. If they were were not inspired "military geniuses" like Alexander, Caesar, Frederick the Great, Napoleon, or Robert E. Lee, the very least that could be said about them was that they were able, conscientious men who knew their business, avoided costly errors, and accomplished their missions.

As for our junior officers, who, almost to the man, were as new to the Army as we selectees were, they either learned fast or were killed fast. They gained invaluable experience in almost impossible terrain during the First Push. Our engineers also distinguished themselves and our Red Legs had shown they could move over, under, or through obstacles as well as shoot. Full use had also been made of our M.G. sections and supporting weapons, as command had insisted. Our S.O.S. was apparently better than in some other divisions. Most importantly, our infantry proved resolute and reliable—they not only possessed doggedness, but also fighting spirit.

True, the Germans in front of us were fighting merely a delaying action, but they were also skilled soldiers who, if they lacked enough infantry for serious counterattacks because they'd been caught napping with their supports on the wrong side of the river, they still fought with efficiency and steadfastness. Every one of their numerous M.G.s, light and heavy, had to be eliminated—at the cost of somebody's life. Through the rain and fog and darkness-drenched woods, out into the open spaces to face the interlocking M.G. fire, with no dry spot on which to rest, we men of the Blue Ridge Division *Always Moved Forward*. If sleep were possible, it was by lying in the rain to wake with fingers so numbed they could not move.

Although our spirit was always good, I think that it was never better than it was at this point in the campaign. For example, cooks insisted that their companies should have hot food, and once done, many asked if they could go out on patrol. Drivers kept their trucks and teams going in spite of shells and mud, still undecided which one was worse. Determination to "help the other fellow," to back him up and to pull one's full weight, was in evidence everywhere.

For the big attack slated for Oct. 4, the division's "Second Push," Cronkhite directed Jamerson's 159th Inf. Brig. (minus 1/318) to attack into Bois d'Ogons with the 318th Infantry (-) on the left and the 317th on the right, in column of battalions (with two companies in front, two in support). Brett's 160th Inf. Brig. was ordered to follow Heiner's 159th Arty. Brig. and be ready to deliver *le coup de grâce*.[37] We in Sweeny's 1/318th Infantry, on the right meanwhile, were instructed to prepare to hand over our hard-won positions in Bois Brieulles to a battalion from the 4th Division in order to eventually join our Blue Ridge brothers who would soon be attacking in the vicinity of Bois d'Ogons, which was to our left front.

Maj. Wise's 2/318th Infantry was to lead the epic attack into Bois d'Ogons up the left flank of the division's axis of advance, followed by 3/318. Lt. Cabell's G/2/318 was on the left, adjoining with members of the 3rd Division and Lt. Lakin's F/2/318 was on the right, connecting with a company from Col. Perry's 317th Infantry Regiment, 80th Division. Companies E and H,

---

[37] *Le coup de grâce* is French for "the final blow" and is pronounced "Lay Coo day Grah."

commanded by Lt. Neubauer and Capt. Moore, respectively, were in support. Like the other battalions, Companies G and F were in front, followed by E and H in support (in combat, we numbered the companies 1, 2, 3, 4 by their position in the line—1 and 2 in the front, with 1 being on the left). Col. Worrilow's P.C. was established in Nantillois itself, about three hundred yards behind 2/318. Lt. Craighill of the 317th Infantry remembered:

> *The colonel, the three majors, and several other officers filed into our trench and we could see by the serious look on all their faces that there was a big job ahead. A rather long discussion ensued, and there was much talk about the time being too short for proper preparation. This talk was useless though, because it had to be done and we were soon told that the regiment was to go over the top the next morning. There was no time to lose—the men had to be gotten ready, orders had to be issued, and many, many details had to be attended to. There was no time for reconnaissance of the ground and without exception the terrain was entirely unfamiliar to all concerned.*[38]

The division M.G. battalions were assigned either barrage or direct support duties. While one M.G. company each was sent to support the assault infantry battalions, the rest were ordered to establish barrage positions atop Hill 295.[39] The division's artillery brigade was ordered to support the infantry attack no later than dawn, Nov. 4. At dusk, Nov. 3 therefore, the brigade, led by Lt. Col. Brunzell's 313th Artillery, departed its firing positions around Hill 281 and headed for Septsarges *via* Gercourt. Preceded by artillery reconnaissance officers, scouts, and markers, Capt. Frank Crandall's E/2/313th Artillery led the brigade move to Nantillois. When the battery moved into an open vale to the north of Hill 281, however, it was immediately struck by a Hun artillery strike from the Heights of the Meuse. One round exploded under the carriage of a gun, badly damaged it, mortally wounded its section chief, and wounded several horses. Battery E then let out at a trot across country toward Septsarges, paralleling Bois Sachet, still under fire and with the wounded horses bleeding badly. Understanding the insanity of moving farther, Capt. Crandall informed Maj. Nash of 2/313th Artillery to turn back and find another route.[40]

---

[38] *317th Infantry*, 61-62.

[39] *Ibid*, 63.

[40] *313th Artillery*, 49.

With this information in hand, Nash decided to weave his batteries, which stretched out to about a km in length, south through the ruins of Béthincourt and then north through Cuisy and into Septsarges where he met with the regimental reconnaissance officers, scouts, and markers who directed the entire regiment to go into battery between Bois Septsarges and Hill 295. According to Lt. Thomas Crowell, the telephone officer of the 313th Artillery:

This was the first and only time that the whole regiment fought from the same position. All the batteries were together, almost in line. 1/313 was echeloned in the western edge of the woods, B and C side by side and A shooting over them. There was excellent cover in the woods and excellent defilade, but the field of fire was limited. 2/313 was located in a little strip of the woods just west of A Battery. They had fine cover and good defilade and a large field of fire. The men had cover in fox-holes near the guns and in parts of an old trench system in Bois Septsarges. Access was good in both positions from roads in rear and excellent echelons were established in Bois Septsarges.[41]

The 313th Artillery was soon joined by its brethren from Walker's 314th and Goodfellow's 315th Artillery, Whitaker's 305th Ammunition Train, and H.Q./155th Arty. Brig. While in this position near Septsarges, the batteries of the brigade were shelled throughout the night of Oct. 3-4 with a hateful mix of gas and H.E. Because of this, the fire direction officers (those who actually calculated the gun solutions) had to plot their up-and-coming barrages while wearing gas masks and the men positioned the guns, dug the trail holes, etc., similarly handicapped. Nobody in the division had had a good night's rest for ten days and nearly all had marched several km under very fatiguing conditions. Most of us had been under direct enemy fire for a about week, which seriously worked on our nerves.

---

[41] As cited in *313th Artillery*, 49-50.

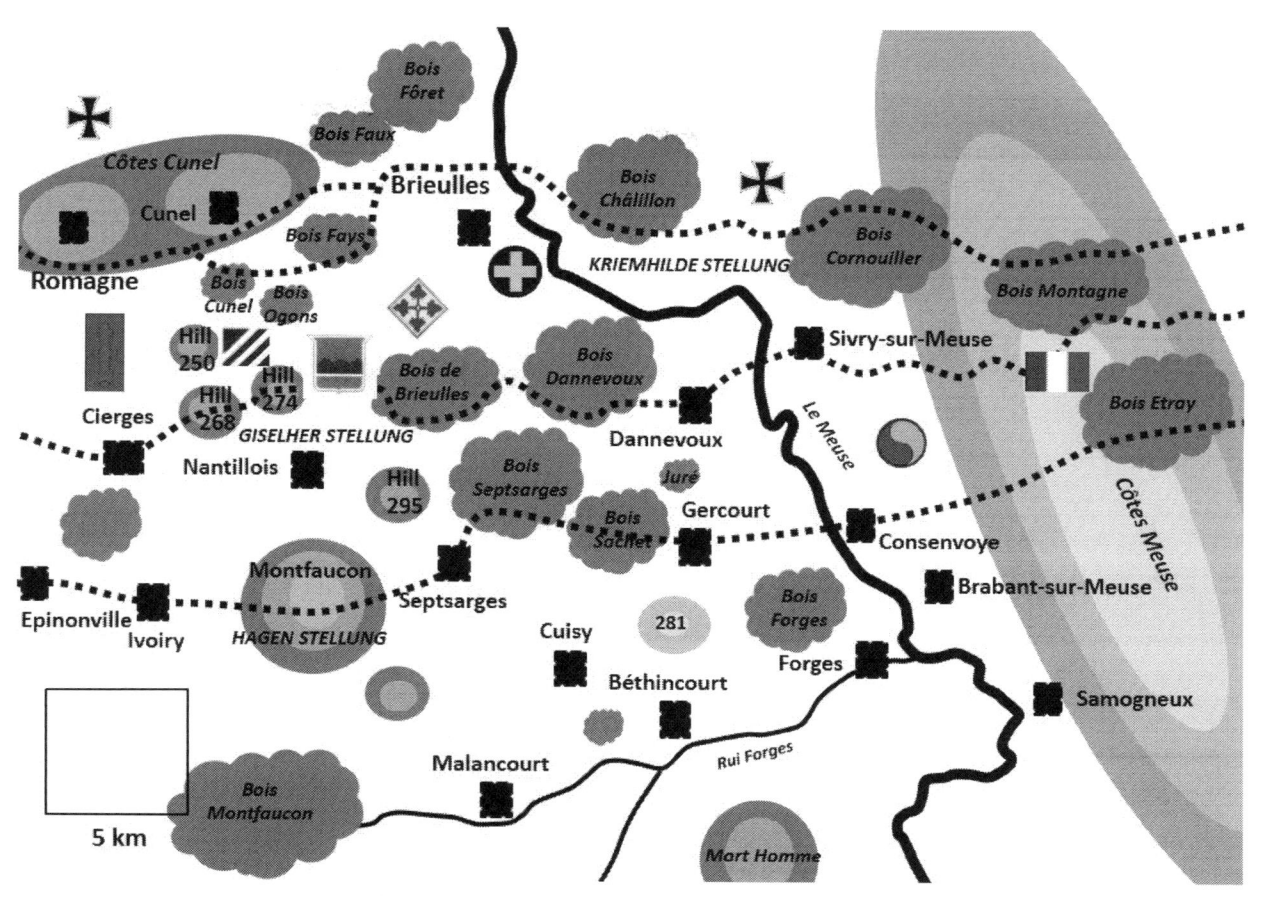

80th Division Area of Operations, Oct. 4, 1918. While the Blue Ridge Division was supposed to attack Bois d'Ogons "Hey-Diddle-Diddle-Right-Up-the-Middle," the 3rd and 4th Divisions were to conduct a double envelopment around its flanks, taking the Heights of Cunel.

The American 3rd, 4th, and 80th Divisions were up against the 5th Bavarian Reserve Division, the 7th Prussian Reserve Division, the 28th Prussian Division, and the 236th Prussian Division.

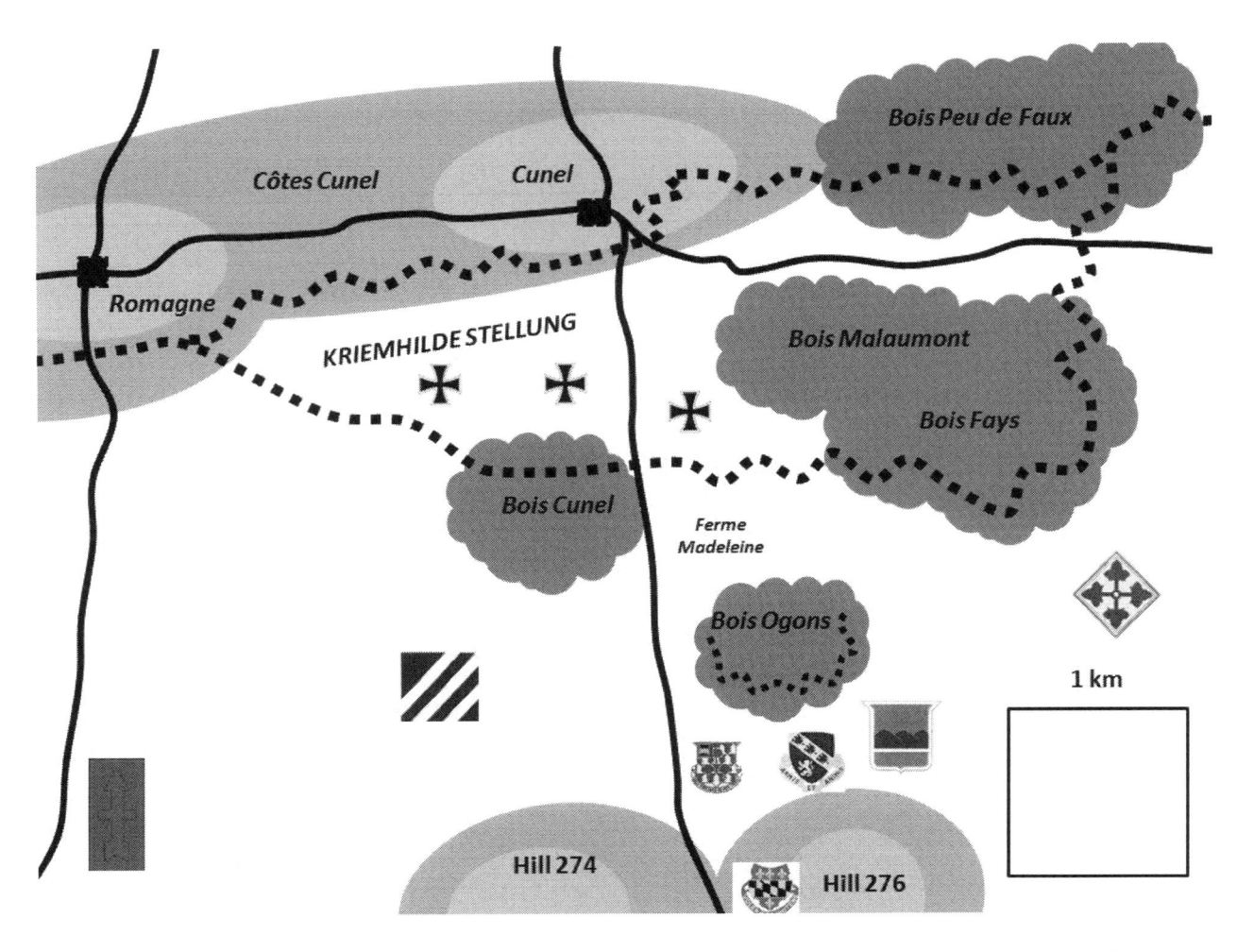

"The Valley of Death" at Ferme Madeleine, Oct. 4, 1918. The 159th Inf. Bde. Was on the attack with the 318th Inf. on the right and the 317th Inf. on the left. The 319th Inf. was in reserve on Hill 276.

Cunel-Nantillois Road looking north (L) and Our attack axis into *Bois d' Ogons* (background) (R). This picture was taken during the winter of 1918-19.

"Bois d'Ogons and slopes to the south."

(L) Cunel-Nantillois Road on right and *Côtes Cunel* in the background. While the 317th Inf. attacked up the right side of the road, the 3rd Inf. Div. up the right. Bois d'Ogons is in the right background of the picture. Ferme Madelaine looking north (R). In the background is Bois Cunel. This place was the bane of our existence.

Hun outpost line being assaulted by Doughs (L) and Pvt. Atherton Clark, L/3/317th Inf., 80th Div. His respirator box is "At the Ready."

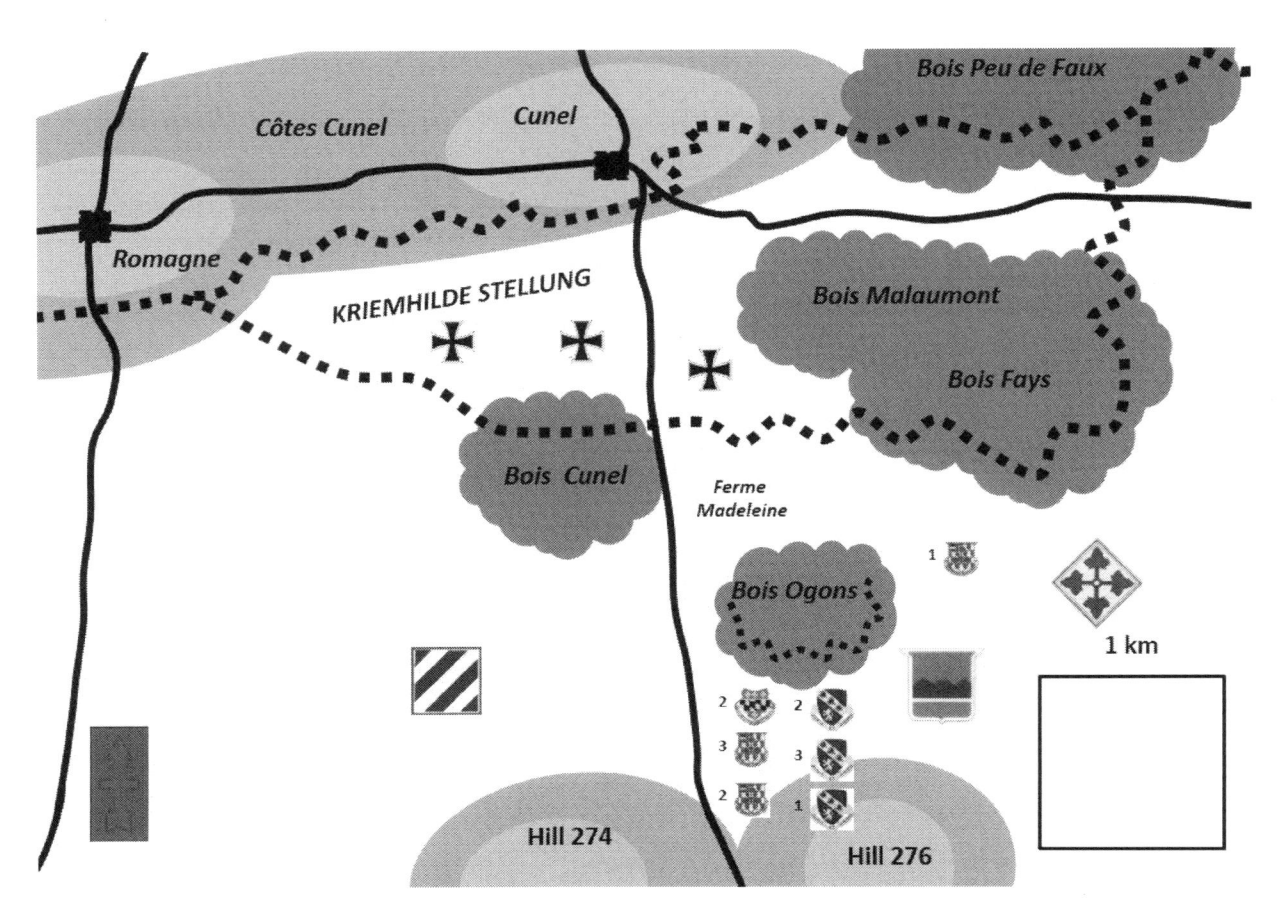

Straight into the belly of the beast, Oct. 5, 1918, A.M. Typical brigade attack with assault, support, and reserve battalions.

La Ferme Madeleine, right in the heart of the "Valley of Death." Bois Cunel is in the background.

for friends & family
$25 OFF

Share this code with friends and family and they'll get **$25 off** their first order with Mixbook!

Code: **FAMBAM** | Expires: 06/30/2019

TERMS: $25 promotional value expires June 30, 2019 11:59pm PT. Limit one per person, per account, per address. Valid online only at Mixbook.com. New customers only. Must use promotional value in one visit. No cash value. Not valid with other promotions or specials. Tax and shipping not included.

THIS CARD IS PRINTED ON MIXBOOK'S SIGNATURE MATTE PAPER.

Mixbook
PHOTO CO.

A LITTLE
SPRING-SPIRATION

Creative Growth Collection
Cards with a cause. 5% of sales go back to artists with disabilities

Desktop Metals
Flat or Curved metal prints

Personalized Kids Books
by Hello!Lucky

Travel Photo Books
J'adore Paris
by Molly Hatch

100% Happiness Guaranteed

We're committed to exceeding your expectations. If you're not completely happy with your order, we'll replace it! Let us know by contacting us at **hello@mixbook.com**.

For more ideas and inspiration visit Mixbook.com/inspiration

"Sunday Morning at Cunel" (L). This captures what it was like for us in Bois d'Ogons and the Valley of Death. "Typical scene in Bois Malaumont" (R). We felt like we were with Bobby Lee in the Wilderness, 1864.

"The French 75" (L) was renown for its rapid firing, "Let's Go!" (C), and "Mosquito Tank in the Ditch" (R). This is what we mostly saw of our tanks.

French Renault "Mosquito" tanks advancing through a bombed-out French ville.

115

"Tank Attack" by Harvey Dunn.

"No Man's Land, 11-1-18." A soldier from the 319th Inf. stands besides a knocked out French Renault tank, objects which we Doughs derisively called "Clank-ity-clanks."

"German Anti-Tank Gun in Firing Position, Oct., 1918" (L) and "German plan forced down near *Cierges*, Oct. 4, 1918" (R).

Chapter 2

The Hell of Bois d'Ogons and *KRIEMHILDE* (October 4-6).

October 4, 1918.

Weather: Rainy.

Roads: Fair.

During the early-morning hours of Oct. 4, Lt. Craighill of the 317th Infantry remembered:

> *The sky was clear but the stars were dimmed as a slight mist hung closely to the ground. The whir of a big bombing machine could be heard far off on its way leaving a wake of utter desolation and destruction. Occasionally the burst of a large shell illuminated the surroundings, and the flash from our guns made one think of a far-off thunder storm with its intermittent flashes of lightning. On and on trudged the long column, struggling over huge heaps of earth thrown up by terrific explosions. Time was creeping on and the leading battalion had not yet reached the designated forming up place.*[42]

On its way north to its assigned attack position, the 317th Infantry got lost.

You heard me right—lost.

This may sound incredible but given the very difficult circumstances, I'm shocked that it didn't actually occur more often.

Lt. Craighill remembered that the regiment "closed up on the Montfaucon-Septsarges Road, just west of Septsarges, and passed through several batteries of French 75s" until it reached the vicinity of Hill 295, which was held by a battalion from the 318th Infantry, the appointed brigade concentration area. "The going was hard—there were numerous thick horny hedges to go through and the grade at this particular juncture was very steep. The fog had gotten pretty thick, making it almost an impossibility to arrive at a true sense of direction." Here the men "cut their blanket rolls loose from the packs, leaving them with only reserve rations and a few necessary toilet articles, and one blanket adjusted in a circular shape, tied around the

---

[42] As cited in *317th Infantry*, 63.

haversack." Gas masks were put in the "alert position" and the "companies formed in platoon columns." Before long, the lead battalion, 2/317, reached the top of the western edge of the hill in the Egyptian darkness and started down the forward slope. At this point, it was decided that they were bearing too far to the left, which was true. The regimental commander, Col. Howard R. Perry, therefore decided to steer more to the right or east. Even then, however, he never made it to the correct concentration area before H-Hour, appreciably under-minding the up-and-coming attack.[43]

The day's objective was the small, blown-up *Village Cunel*, which stood atop a low-lying ridge north of Bois d'Ogons. This doesn't sound like much, but we were, in fact, supposed to break the strongest defensive line of the vaunted *HINDENBURG STELLUNG*: *KRIEMHILDE*. Each Infantry platoon was to advance using as much cover and concealment as possible. Individual soldier initiative and fitness to move forward with his rifle, bayonet, and grenades, was essential. Once a platoon was knocked out due to casualties or sheer exhaustion, a following platoon would take its place. As many M.G. sections as possible would be pressed forward. We were told that the area in question was held by the Prussian 236th Infantry Division.

They have 236 divisions!?

At 5:35 A.M., a rolling barrage delivered by the 155th Artillery Brigade kicked off the attack., targeting *KRIEMHILDE* between Bois d'Ogons and Cunel. About fifteen minutes later, the Hun answered with a counter-barrage, which, for once, made ours seem like that of a small boy. It was bad. Scores of Blue Ridgers were either blown to bits or buried beneath the vomiting earth.

At 6:00 A.M., 2/318 crossed the L.D. north of Nantillois and advanced two kms up the axis of advance—guiding on the right or east side of the Cunel-Nantillois Road—and pushed into Bois d'Ogons by 7:30 A.M., following the barrage line. Company F was on the right and Company G was on the left, using the road as a guide, with E and H in support. Behind them was 3/318.[44]

Perry's 317th Infantry, which was supposed to attack in conjunction with the 318th Infantry, was nowhere to be found, as it was still making its way over from the left, and some of

---

[43] *317th Infantry*, 63.

[44] *318th Infantry*, 172.

the divisional M.G. sections were still coming up from the south.[45] Because of this, the right flank of the 318th Infantry was exposed, although we in 1/318 were holding the left flank of Bois Brieulles.

It was hoped that Bois d'Ogons would simply be out-posted—that the "rough stuff" would start only once we began to cross the open fields of *Ferme Madeleine* and frontally assault *KRIEMHILDE* between Bois Cunel and Fay. That's where command thought we'd suffer 50% or more casualties and they were already calling it the "Valley of Death," hearkening back to the accursed area between Little Round Top and Devil's Den at the Battle of Gettysburg. There, it was thought, we'd hand the battle over to Lt. Col. James Love's 319th Infantry of Brett's 160th Inf. Brig. and they would deliver *le côup de grace*, breach the line, and seize the heights.

That was the plan, anyway.

The hopes of the men of 2/318 were soon dashed, however, when it learned that Bois d'Ogons was in fact strongly held by the Hun and those woods became THE absolute bane of our existence—the defining days of our many months in France. One can plainly see how our first attack failed by reading the message traffic. At 7:35 A.M., Maj. Wise, commander of 2/318 (HATFIELD) sent the following message to Col. Worrilow, commander of 318th Infantry (HAMMOND): "HAMMOND, this is HATFIELD: No signs of HARPER [317th Infantry]. I am enfiladed three ways by machine guns." At 7:50 A.M.: "HAMMOND, this is HATFIELD: Held up by machine guns in Ogons Woods, rear slope, under observation and heavy shelling. You must turn wood from right or left."[46]

With Perry's 317th Infantry still coming up from the left, Col. Worrilow moved 3/318 from reserve and deployed it to the right of 2/318. But still, the 318th Infantry could not advance, the German line being too strong and the thick woods of Bois d'Ogons impeding the effective use of A.R.s, R.G.s, I.G.s, M.G.s, or mortars, let alone artillery. At 8:15 A.M., B/1/314th Artillery, the 317th Infantry's accompanying battery, could only get as far north as the back side of Hill 274, where it went into position on the right side of the road and established an O.P. on top of the hill. According to one soldier from the 314th Artillery: "The infantry had not met with the hoped-for success nor were they anywhere near Cunel… Capt. Graves was told that the infantry had no

---

[45] *317th Infantry*, 65.

[46] As cited in *318th Infantry*,

mission for him and his battery was returned to 1/314 in the afternoon."[47] We all later believed that the first attack through Bois d'Ogons failed for the following reasons:

1. The 317th Infantry (HARPER) was unsuccessful in crossing the line of departure (L.D.) at the same time as the 318th Infantry (HAMMOND), thus leaving 2/318 (HATFIELD's) right flank "in the air."

2. The Rock of the Marne Division also failed to advance as expected, leaving HATFIELD's left flank "in the air."

3. The exposure of both of 2/318's flanks made it necessary to throw out strong flank guard detachments from 3/318 (HANSCOM) and involved them in the attack much earlier than should have been necessary.

4. The failure of flanking units to advance resulted in Companies F and G of 2/318 being ripped to pieces by German M.G. fire not only from front, but also from both flanks.

5. Being at the apex of a triangle, Hun artillery delivered massive artillery against 2/318, which had its neck stuck far-out in Bois d'Ogons.

The inevitable result was that Maj. Wise's 2/318th Infantry suffered very heavy casualties, including the major himself, and its battered remnants fell back to the L.D., which was held by H.Q./318. This first attack into Bois d'Ogons cost 2/318 all of its company commanders and 60% of its remaining officers were made *hors de combat*. Everyone blamed Col. Perry, the commander of the 317th Infantry.

Fair? Probably not, but that's just the way it is.

During this day's battle, Pvt. Eddie Baum of M/3/318th Infantry earned the D.S.C. His citation reads:

For extraordinary heroism in action in the BOIS OGONS, France, 4 October, 1918. Private Baum was acting as a stretcher bearer with another soldier who was shot by a sniper. Going out under fire from the sniper, he captured the latter with the aid of another man. While taking his prisoner to the rear, Private

---

[47] As cited in *314th Artillery*, 39.

Baum found a wounded man whom he carried to the aid station under heavy fire, while his companion went on with the prisoner. Upon returning from the aid station he continued his work of rescuing the wounded. [48]

To make matters even worse for us, believe it or not, Hun artillery attacks launched from *les Côtes de Meuse* (yes, still!) continued throughout the day. These types of attacks are especially trying to troop morale, especially when they come from one's right flank or right rear as it gives troops the feeling that they are being fired upon by their own artillery. Soon after noon, 2/318 sent the following message: "HAMMOND to HAROLD [159th Inf. Brig.]: Request counter-battery work on batteries east of the Meuse."[49]

I say again: the battle for Bois d'Ogons Oct. 4-6, 1917, was the most challenging of all of our fights—it was hell on earth—the Devil's Cauldron. The 159th Inf. Brig. had already suffered some 40% casualties since it crossed the L.D. on Sept. 26 and how we were actually going to punch through that witch-bitch *KRIEMHILDE* near Cunel we did not know. In fact, we all thought we were going to die and then a follow-on division would move in and take all the glory.

With the attack stalled at Bois d'Ogons, Cronkhite (HAMILTON) ordered the one battalion from Brett's 160th Inf. Brig. to be sent forward to support the attack of Jamerson's 159th Inf. Brig. The selected battalion was Maj. James Montague's 2/319th Infantry (white circles on their helmets and code-named "HALIBUT"), which was stationed atop Hill 295 with the regiment's supporting weapons. HALIBUT was attached to the 318th Infantry to take the place of we in 1/318, which was still operating in Bois Brieulles with the Ivy Division. At 3:45 P.M., Cronkhite sent the following message to 3/319: "HALIBUT, this is HAMILTON: Move into HAROLD sector. Two companies in first wave, two in second. Pass through HATFIELD and HANSCOM and attack Bois Ogons following barrage, which will start at 4:30 P.M."[50]

In moving forward, Montague's 2/319 was strafed by a German aeroplane near Hill 295. As the plane looped around for a second run, however, it was brought down by some "Archies" and crash-landed into a camouflaged battery of the 314th Artillery, which suffered no casualties. Shortly after, another Hun aeroplane was brought down in a similar fashion, but this one

---

[48] As cited in *318th Infantry*, 69.

[49] As cited in *318th Infantry*, 172.

[50] *Ibid*, 173.

completely collapsed and caught fire before it hit the ground.[51] Lt. Furr of the 314th M.G. remembered:

> *Both the Allied and German air fleets showed great activity that morning—four German planes were brought down within an hour. German plans swept low, machine-gunning the railroad cut and the hill on which the battalion was located and incidentally stirring up everyone in the vicinity to take a shot back at them—"Archies," M.G.s and the "Doughboy" with his rifle.*[52]

The second attack against Bois d'Ogons was launched soon after 4:30 P.M. with 1/317 on the right and 2/319 on the left. In 2/319, Capt. Herr's Company F was on the right and Capt. Keezel's Company H was on the left as the attack companies. 3/318 was in support of 2/319 and the now-decimated 2/318 was in reserve. For the 317th Infantry, 2/317 was support and 3/317 was reserve.

This second attack also failed to break the German line, although 2/319 did make some advances through the dark and accursed wood, which was still defended by scores of Hun M.G. teams—and very adept snipers. Lt. Craighill of 2/317th Infantry reported:

> *The first wave was met by very heavy M.G. and artillery fire from the north, northeast, and east and part of this fire enfiladed our lines and only a few of our troops succeeded in reaching the edge of the Bois de Ogons. No further advance could be made beyond this position during the day. In addition to the H.E. and shrapnel used by the enemy, he also threw over a great many gas shells in the vicinity of Nantillois and the ravines around the town.*[53]

The key to advancing against dug-in *Boche* M.G. positions was to find holes or fissures in their line, through the woods and under the brush. While the R.G. and A.R. squad, reinforced by M.G.s, I.G.s, or even direct fire light artillery pieces, held the German M.G. positions in front, gaining *fire superiority*, the bomber and assault squad would maneuver closer to the left or right and try to find a point to assault through. I cannot emphasize the concept of *gaining fire*

---

[51] *2/319th Infantry*, 10.

[52] *314th M.G.*, 40.

[53] *317th Infantry*, 65.

superiority before you maneuver onto an objective enough. Starting with your A.R.s and R.G.s and culminating with your M.G.s, blanket the target with converging fire—dominate it like a fire fighter puts out a fire with a high-powered hose. Only then, under the cover of smoke, should you send your assault units forward. If you can't see the target, then keep on firing until you do. If you run out of ammunition, command will simply send up another unit to take your place while you get replenished.

Due to the terrain and other factors, companies and battalions could not advance as one—only platoons could. As such, the threat of so-called "friendly fire" was great in Bois d'Ogons. Every time a Hun darted through the brush, for example, an attacking Dough thought that he might be a fellow from another company. Hence a challenge was usually made before firing.

This saved the life of many-a-Hun.

To break the stalemate, Jamerson's 159th Inf. Brig. would have to somehow get a light battery from Heiner's 155th Arty. Brig., with support from Spalding's 305th Engineers, up into Bois d'Ogons in order to blast the Hun M.G. positions with direct fire. As of yet, Capt. Robert Perkins of B/313th Artillery, which was the accompanying battery for Perry's 317th Infantry and Capt. Lester Graves's C/314th Artillery, which was the accompanying battery Worrilow's 318th Infantry, believed that the terrain alone would not enable them to get their guns up there. And if they tried, they'd be sitting ducks and would be quickly destroyed by artillery fire from the Heights of the Meuse. This meant that more M.G.s ("Jackass Artillery") would somehow have to get up into the accursed woods. With that in mind, at 8:00 P.M., Maj. Robert Cox's 314th M.G. Battalion (Mot.) received orders from General Jamerson stating that it was to join the 319th Infantry and other M.G. sections that were taking up defensive positions south of Nantillois. Once Cox arrived to the position, he learned that because the attack had been stalled and that the 318th Infantry had been punched in the face, more units of the 319th Infantry would be sent north to support them and that the 314th M.G. Battalion would be part of this particular operation.[54]

---

[54] *314th M.G.*, 40.

October 5, 1918.

Weather: Clear.

Roads: Fair.

Due to the mix-ups, which directly led to the 80th Division's failure to take Bois d'Ogons on Oct. 4, Col. Perry of the 317th Infantry was relieved of command by General Cronkhite and replaced by Lt. Col. Charles Keller, the regimental X.O. At about 4:00 A.M. Oct. 5, in the cold, wet, inky-black darkness, we in 1/318 (Red Squares) finally reached the 159th Inf. Brig.'s sector southeast of Bois d'Ogons and prepared to support our brigade's attack into it by advancing through Bois Fays in conjunction with units from the 4th Division.[55] With this move, battalions from Worrilow's 318th Infantry would now be positioned on both flanks of the 159th Inf. Brig., the 80th Division. At 5:30 A.M. Maj. Montague of 2/319 reported to Col. Worrilow: "Battalion in woods with elements of 317th and 318th. Unable to mop up M.G.s. Have no support left."[56]

Even though the infantry regiments of the 80th Division were now below 50% strength, Bullard, our corps commander, ordered us to renew our attack against *KRIEMHILDE* anyway. He apparently did not care (or was ordered not to care) about the condition of his troops and insisted that we fixed bayonets and attack the enemy no matter what. Jamerson's 159th Inf. Brig. would therefore once again attack up the right side of the Cunel-Nantillois Road and into Bois d'Ogons. To its right was the 4th Division and to its left was the 3rd Division. We in the 80th Division were supposed to pin or hold the Germans in front while the 3rd and 4th Divisions conducted a double-envelopment against the heights. Just as General Lee told his corps commanders at Gettysburg on July 3, 1863—"The general plan of the attack remains unchanged"—the same held true for us. Behind us were the infantry and M.G. companies of the 160th Inf. Brig. and the firing batteries of our artillery brigade.

Before dawn, Cronkhite, with Bullard breathing down his neck, sent the following message to Jamerson, commander of the 159th Inf. Brig.: "The reputation of the division is at stake. Ogons Wood must be taken!" We later learned that Bullard said to Cronkhite, and I quote: "Give up the attack and you are a goner—you'll lose your command in 24 hours!" Generals apparently like to yell at each other, as that's apparently how they communicate.

---

[55] *Bois Fays* is pronounced "Bwa Fay."

[56] As cited Stultz, 439.

Shortly after dawn, Jamerson, backed by artillery from Heiner's brigade, ordered the attack battalions of Jamerson's 159th Inf. Brig. to renew their advance north through Bois d'Ogons and Fays with the ultimate objective of breaching *KRIEMHILDE* at what was left of the tiny Cunel. Once the 3rd, 80th, and 4th Divisions broke through *KRIEMHILDE* at Cunel, it was hoped, the American First Army would only have one more line to breach and then, after that, we would finally pass into the "Open Warfare" phase that would more than likely force the Imperial German Government to surrender. As usual, the attack started with an artillery barrage. According to Lt. Thomas Crowell, the Telephone Officer of the 313th Artillery: "Preparation fire was delivered from about 5:00 to 6:00 A.M. and a rolling barrage from 6:00 to 8:00 A.M. with 50 meter jumps at three minute intervals."[57]

During this particular attack, the third against Bois d'Ogons in two days, we in 1/318th Infantry were to seize the western boundary of Bois Fays and continue the attack into Bois Malaumont. 1/318 was on the right, 2/317 was in the center, and 2/319 was on the left, using the Cunel-Nantillois Road as its left guide. Behind 2/319, 3/318 was in support with 2/318 in reserve. Behind them were the remaining infantry battalions of the 319th and 320th Infantry of Brett's 160th Inf. Brig., as well as several divisional M.G. sections, namely from Cox's 314th M.G. Battalion (Mot.).[58] During the artillery preparation, Col. Welsh, the Operations Officer for the 155th Arty. Brig., directed Lt. Col. Walker of the 314th Artillery "to transmit orders for cooperation to a French battalion of 75s which were in position near 2/314." The French commander informed Walker that he could "take no orders coming through such channels," however, and the attack was deprived of an entire battalion of field guns.[59]

Speaking of French support, the attack of Maj. Montague's 2/319 on the division's left was supposed to be supported by three French Renault "Mosquito" Tanks that were armed with Hotchkiss air-cooled heavy M.G.s. The tanks were to advance straight up the Cunel-Nantillois Road between Hill 274 and Bois d'Ogons and seize Ferme Madelaine. The Mosquito Tanks were quickly taken out by massed Hun artillery, however, and their crews bolted to the rear. This is one reason why we called tanks "Clink-it-ty-Clanks" (aside from the sound their caterpillar tracks made when moving). Lt. Higgins of 3/318th Infantry, in the leading company of the support battalion, remembered seeing the French tank crews streaming back to the rear down

---

[57] As cited in *313th Artillery*, 51.

[58] *314th M.G.*, 40.

[59] *314th Artillery*, 39.

the road. Thinking that they were in fact Germans who had slipped through the lines, he hurled a hand grenade at them "which completely deranged what little morale the crews retained."[60] Before long, he realized who the men really were, and off they disappeared through the thick smoke and fog to the south.

We believe that the main reason why the Hun artillery was so accurate in the sector, aside from the fact they had lived here for years and had every square meter plotted out (!), was that several parallel lines of telegraph poles ran over Hill 274, enabling the Hun to adjust their fire upon the reverse slopes with great accuracy. Hun aeroplanes also continued to fly about at will, directing fire and, from low altitudes, sweeping the rear slope clear of our boys with their M.G.s. One of these "motored kites" even dropped propaganda leaflets upon us, which explained to us "How to Stop the War" by surrendering to the Kaiser. I don't know how effective the leaflets were, but I don't know of anybody who actually crossed over to German lines.

Unable to maintain communication between battalion and regimental H.Q., due to constant cutting of the field telephone wire and runner casualties from enemy M.G.s, the 2/318's P.C. was moved back to a pit at the rear base of Hill 274 where the enemy had maintained a M.G. nest. But even here it was difficult to maintain command and control. The large number of wounded who sought the cover of the pit and other traffic soon attracted the attention of the hostile planes which twice fired directly into the command post. Several of the wounded there were killed by shrapnel.

At 10:00 A.M., we in 1/318th Infantry began our attack into Bois Fays. After advancing some five hundred yards further into the dark, wet woods, we discovered abandoned German barracks that were arranged like little gnome villages. I for one was awestruck by the boardwalks running through the woods from one building to another and the carefully tended gardens that were planted among them. The surreal peace of "Gnome City" didn't last long, however, as concealed German Maxim M.G.s and snipers opened fire on us, slicing up several officers and men. Huge *Minenwerfer* H.E. rounds ("G.I. Cans") followed the M.G. bullets.

"Shew, crrupp!"

"Rat-a-tat-a-tat!"

"Rat-a-tat-a-tat!"

---

[60] *318th Infantry*, 68.

"Rat-a-tat-a-tat!"

"Shew, crrupp!"

"Rat-a-tat-a-tat!"

We were once again getting plastered and took cover in a nearby dip in the woods. We fixed bayonets and waited for a Hun counter-attack that never came.

"Shew, crrupp!"

"Rat-a-tat-a-tat!"

"Rat-a-tat-a-tat!"

"Rat-a-tat-a-tat!"

Scream.

Faced with this nasty attack, we pulled back in order to get more men. During this action, Sergeant William T. Johnson, A/1/318th Infantry, was later awarded the D.S.C. for "extraordinary heroism." His citation read:

> *For extraordinary heroism in action in the BOIS DE FAYS, France, 5 October, 1918. While leading a patrol Sergeant Johnson encountered terrific machine gun fire, which forced him to order his patrol to cover. He then advanced alone, working his way to the nest which he destroyed, and allowed for the continuance of the patrol. Later the same day he braved the perils of an extremely heavy barrage to bring to safety a wounded comrade who was lying 300 yards in advance of the lines.*[61]

At about noon, an Archie and a gas and flame section from the American III Corps, placed at the disposal of General Jamerson, arrived to Hill 274. Like the French tanks, their arrival brought down a terrific fire from the German artillery.

Jamerson therefore ordered them out.

---

[61] As cited in *318th Infantry*, 70.

With their withdrawal, the fire abated somewhat, though the enemy continued to "crash" the position periodically with several "battery one's" (the artillery battery fires one round per gun), including a heavy battery from the right rear beyond the Meuse. To the observers of these Hun batteries the rear crest of Hill 274 was apparently plainly visible. With our attack stalled, at around 2:30 P.M., our own artillery shellacked the strong German positions north of Bois d'Ogons and Fays with H.E. and shrapnel so that Jamerson's 159th Inf. Brig. could once again claw its way forward, eliminating Hun M.G. nests one-by-one in the all-too-familiar, bloody fashion.

During these "lulls" or "operational pauses," we Doughs were generally assigned to help evacuate the wounded, bring up ammunition or other supplies, etc. Those of us not so engaged, would usually smoke or chew tobacco or ate canned (or corned) beef and crackers to help sooth our nerves and to occupy our minds. Sometimes, we'd even read old letters—anything to take our minds off the terror that was unfolding around us. But despite all of these "diversions," we were still 100% wired to tell when the next round or the next bullet was going sail into our position, making minced meat of any of us.

On the far-left, near the road, Capt. Herr's F/2/319 of Maj. Montague's infantry battalion suffered a direct hit by an enemy artillery strike, "wounding several men and causing some of those near to temporarily lose their sense of direction and consequently were separated from the company and were taken prisoner."[62] These Doughs were held by the Germans for three months as prisoners of war (P.O.W.s), after the Armistice was signed in mid-November. (See Appendix 2 on their P.O.W. experience.) Montague's battalion surgeon, Lt. James R. St. Clair, who had followed F/2/319 into the fight, also became separated after the devastating strike. He actually made his way out of the woods with Company F's Bugler, Pvt. Michael A. Cerra, but was soon driven into a water-filled shell hole by Hun M.G. fire from Hill 250. Every time St. Clair and Cerra tried to exit the hole, the Heinies opened up on them from the hill. These two men were pinned for eighteen hours until a patrol from the Rock of the Marne Division stumbled upon them on Oct. 6.[63]

With this attack thrown back, what was left of 2/319th Infantry assembled along the reverse slope of Hill 276, which was the regiment's L.D. There they dug-in with their intrenching

---

[62] As cited in *2/319th Infantry*, 11.

[63] *2/319th Infantry*, 11.

tools, tried to eat and sleep, and posted sentries, all under constant enemy M.G. and artillery fire. It was "one bloody hell of a mess," for sure.

Being pinned, for any amount of time, makes a person feel helpless and worthless and when it occurred, we begged God for relief.

"To get the attack moving again," Bullard stormed in the H.Q.s of his divisions, including that of the 80th Division, and demanded a resumption of the attack. After his one-sided meeting with Cronkhite, Bullard issued the following directive:

```
1. Give orders for Jamerson to reorganize at once for another effort.

2. Give him a barrage and let him follow it closely and make another attack this afternoon, at an hour to be fixed by you.

3. Organize a good barrage for him.

4. The best information obtainable from the 3d Division, its right located in the woods containing Hill 250, southwest of BOIS DES OGONS. Report efforts being made to clean up this wood. They may have small detachment in vicinity of CUNEL-BOIS CUNEL. Not cleaned up on our right flank. 4th Division holding west side BOIS FAYS and BOIS FAUX on the north, line about 200 yards south of CUNEL-BRIEULLES ROAD. Eastern side of BOIS DE FAYS and BOIS DE FAUX thickly wooded and may not be penetrated by men.

                                                          -BULLARD
```

Generally, it is bad form (and practice) to tell a subordinate commander "how" to do a job. It's best to simply tell him what to do and resource his "how." If, however, you lack confidence in your subordinate, then it is appropriate, due to time-constraints, to tell him not only what to do, but how to do it. If this situation occurs—that you feel the need to tell a subordinate commander how to do it—then said subordinate commander should be replaced at the earliest possible moment. If, however, you feel the need to exhibit tight control, you'll be considered being a "micro-manager" or a "martinet," or a "puppet master," all of which hold negative connotations. During the Meuse-Argonne Offensive, Pershing did become a martinet of sorts, as did Bullard. At times, Bullard would issues orders to brigades or even battalions without going through the chain of command (e.g., through Cronkhite). This is a mistake because once this is done, then the subordinate commander, in this case, a division commander, has just lost control of his unit in battle. Is it appropriate to tell a division commander: "Take Hill 546"? Yes. But not, "Order 1/319th Infantry to swing to the left, 2/320th Infantry to the right, etc." That's a division and/or brigade commander's job. Anyway, Cronkhite's subsequent directions to Jamerson were as follows:

```
Starting from X ravine south of BOIS DES OGONS, under cover of barrage
to be arranged by you with Welsh at earliest possible hour move
forward as directed and make every effort possible to establish and
hold a line in the northern part of BOIS DES OGONS. Urge upon
regimental and battalion commanders the importance of this effort
which must be successful if it is possible to make it so, and proceed
with the reorganization of battalions in the rear. Every possible use
should be made of tanks at your disposal. Use the gas company that
reported to you last night. The line established by you must be
reorganized in depth to the special view to protecting both your
flanks. 4th Division was subjected to a heavy counter-attack this
morning, which may be repeated. The 4th Division is receiving fire
from the northeast, probably from the TRANCHEE DE TETON as well as
from BRIEULLES.

                                                         -CRONKHITE
```

The difficulties confronted by General Jamerson and his staff at this time were increased by incorrect information supplied by Bullard's Chief of Staff, Brig. Gen. Alfred W. Bjornstad. In his eagerness to move the corps forward, disregarding standard procedure (i.e., using the chain of command by contacting the 80th Division's chief of staff), the corps chief telephoned the brigade commanders directly, insisting that their units were "lagging." Convinced by careful reconnaissances that the 3rd and 4th Divisions were not where Bjornstad had told him where they were, Jamerson contacted the commander of the 7th Inf. Brig., 4th Division himself. The latter informed him that units of the 7th Inf. Brig., 4th Division, were in fact farther south than what the American III Corps believed or hoped. Informed of this by Jamerson, Cronkhite determined to end this non-regulation practice right then and there. Accordingly, he insisted henceforth that all orders, instructions, and/or information for the 80th Division be transmitted directly to division H.Q. and never again to his brigades. The protest of General Cronkhite and his chief of staff, Col. Waldron, naturally did not make them popular at corps H.Q., but they didn't care, as they were "Rough and Regular" and comfortable in their skins.

Once the doctrinally incorrect practice of micro-management was fixed, the next attack was set for 6 P.M. By the time battalion commanders, summoned about 4:30 P.M., had received their instructions at regimental headquarters and returned to their commands, however, they only had about thirty minutes to prepare for the push which would be made across the entire divisional front. This time, battalions from the French 228th Artillery Regiment would join in the barrage.

At 6:00 P.M., the division's fourth attack in two days into Bois d'Ogons, commenced behind another rolling barrage. We in 1/318th Infantry led out on the right, attaining the southwest corner of Bois Fays while 2/317th Infantry attacked into Bois d'Ogons in the center and the 2/319th Infantry attacked into the accursed woods on the left. Of all the battalions, Montague's 2/319, had the hardest time of it and suffered far more casualties than we did on the right in Bois Fays. Montague attacked with Capt. Herr's shot-up Company F on the right, Capt. Keezell's Company H on the left, and Companies E and G in support. Behind them was 2/318, followed by 3/318. Col. Worrilow expressly directed that Hill 274 was not to be uncovered until Maj. Montague had made good his hold upon the wood. In 2/318, Lts. Lakin, Ulrich, and Atkinson commanded the first wave, and Lts. Davidson and Crocker commanded the second wave, composed of only about 100 men.

What really hurt Montague's battalion was that soon after the attack was launched, a friendly barrage fell upon his lead companies, followed by enemy barrage. Nevertheless, Maj. Montague was able to get his battalion across the swale and into the wood before enemy M.G.s really started cutting meat. Luckily for the men of Montague's 2/319, the Huns had withdrawn from the damned woods and pulled back to Côtes Cunel and *KRIEMHILDE,* leaving but a small rear-guard. At 7:15 P.M., Maj. Montague sent the following message to Col. Worrilow: "HALIBUT [2/319] entered woods in good order, following barrage."[64] Capt. Charles R. Herr of F/2/319 remembered:

---

[64] As cited Stultz, 442.

We hugged the barrage, making use of all available cover against the M.G. fire. For a space of three hundred yards we moved down a hill, coming across a small stream and up the other slope facing the fire of the enemy over perfectly open ground. Thanks to the shell holes our casualties were few. We followed the barrage through the woods until our objective was reached where we started to dig in at once. [65]

By 8:30 P.M., well after dark, Montague's 2/319th Infantry finally reached the northern edge of Bois d'Ogons. There they peered through the darkness across the open fields to barely discern Ferme Madelaine and Côtes Cunel in the moonlight. Montague ordered F and H/2/319th Infantry to advance to the bombed-out farmstead. Capt. Keesell's H/2/319th Infantry became misdirected in the dark woods, however, (no surprise!) and did not advance as far as Capt. Herr's F/2/319. One of Keesell's platoons was in fact "lost" for several hours. To hear Capt. Herr of Pittsburgh tell it: "Company F was pressing on when M.G. fire burst upon it and, failing to find friendly troops on the left, changed direction in order to get back to the rest of the battalion. As the men were doing this, a grenade burst among them, scattering them. Since it was impossible to reorganize under the intense fire in the dark, the order was given to follow in file across the road, into Bois Cunel, which was still enemy-held, in the 3rd Division's area."[66] It was 10 A.M. next day before the survivors—three officers and thirty men—got back across the road, returning to the battalion. Montague's 2/319 suffered almost 50% casualties in Bois d'Ogons, pretty much making it *hors de combat* for the rest of the battle.

Faced with these stunning losses, Montague ordered his remaining companies, E and G/2/319, to consolidate their position 200 yards back from the northern wood line of Bois d'Ogons, to evade intense enemy M.G. and artillery fire delivered from *KRIEMHILDE*. Once situated, Montague gave the command "defend." According to the *I.D.R.*:

Defense.

498. Supports are posted as close to the firing line as practicable and reinforce the latter according to the principles explained in the attack. When natural cover is not sufficient for the purpose, communicating and cover trenches are constructed. If time does not permit their construction, it is better to begin the

---

[65] As cited in *2/319th Infantry*, 11.

[66] *Ibid.*

action with a very dense firing line and no immediate supports than to have supports greatly exposed in rear.

499. The reserve should be posted so as to be entirely free to act as a whole, according to the developments. The distance from firing line to reserve is generally greater than in the attack. By reason of such a location the reserve is best able to meet a hostile enveloping attack; it has a better position from which to make a counter attack—it is in a better position to cover a withdrawal and permit an orderly retreat. The distance from firing line to reserve increases with the size of the reserve.

500. When the situation is no longer in doubt, the reserve should be held in rear of the flank which is most in danger or offers the best opportunity for counterattack. Usually the same flank best suits both purposes.

501. In exceptional cases, on broad fronts, it may be necessary to detach a part of the reserve to protect the opposite flank. This detachment should be the smallest consistent with its purely protective mission.

502. The commander assigns to subordinates the front to be occupied by them. These, in turn, subdivide the front among their next lower units in the firing line.

503. An extended position is so divided into sections that each has, if practicable, a field of fire naturally made distinct by the terrain. Unfavorable and unimportant ground will ordinarily cause gaps to exist in the line.

504. The size of the unit occupying each section depends upon the latter's natural strength, front, and importance. If practicable, battalions should be kept intact and assigned as units to sections or parts of sections.

505. Where important dead space lies in front of one section, an adjoining section should be instructed to cover it with fire when necessary, or machine guns should be concealed for the like purpose.

507. Unless the difficulty of moving the troops into the position be great, most of the troops of the firing line are held in rear of it until the infantry attack begins. The position itself is occupied by a small garrison only, with the necessary out guards or patrols in front.

508. Fire alone can not be depended upon to stop the attack. The troops must be determined to resort to the bayonet, if necessary.

509. If a night attack or close approach by the enemy is expected, troops in a prepared position should strengthen the out guards and firing line and construct as numerous and effective obstacles as possible. Supports and local reserves should move close to the firing line and should, with the firing line, keep bayonets fixed. If practicable, the front should be illuminated, preferably from the flanks of the section.

510. Only short range fire is of any value in resisting night attacks. The bayonet is the chief reliance. (See Night Operations.)

Theory of the Defensive.[67]

The defense is divided into the purely passive defense and the active defense. The passive defense seeks merely to delay the enemy. The results can never be other than negative. It is usually for the purpose of gaining time and most frequently used by a rear guard. Since the idea of taking up the offensive is absent, no strong reserves are held out for a counter-attack—the firing line is as strong as possible from the first; every advantage is taken of obstacles, natural or artificial. The flanks must be made secure. The active defense seeks to attack the other side at some stage of the engagement. It seeks to win and only the offensive wins. It is often necessary for a commander to assume the defensive (active) either voluntarily, in order to gain time, or to secure some advantage over the enemy; or involuntarily, as in a meeting engagement where the enemy gets a start in deployment for action or where the enemy's attack is impetuous and without sufficient preparation. In either case the defensive force contents

---

[67] *P.M.*, 248.

itself with parrying the blows of the enemy, while gathering and arranging its strength, looking and waiting for the right place and time to deliver a decisive blow which is called the counter-attack. Hence, a counter-attack is the offensive movement of an active defense. Its success greatly depends on being delivered with vigor and at the proper time. It may be delivered in two ways: 1st, straight to the front against a weak point in the attacking line, or 2d, by launching reserves against the enemy's flank after he is fully committed to the attack. The latter method offers the greatest chances for success and the most effective results.

Advantages and Disadvantages of The Defensive.[68]

The defense has the following advantages over the attack:

1. Troops attacking afford a better target than the troops of the defensive.

2. A larger amount of ammunition is usually available.

3. The men shoot better because they are not fatigued by advancing.

4. Losses will be less if good cover is secured.

The defense has the following disadvantages over the attack:

1. The defender surrenders the advantage of the initiative as the attacker can elect the point of attack and the defender must be prepared at all points.

2. The defender must fight amidst his dead and wounded, which is depressing.

3. The defender, seeing the enemy continually advancing, becomes conscious of his inability to stop him. This is depressing to the defender and is injurious to his morale.

---

[68] *P.M.,* 249.

The Passive Defense.

F.S.R. 184. A force may at times fully accomplish its mission by retaining its position for a specified time with or without combat. Here the object is to avoid giving the enemy the decision, either by avoiding combat altogether or, if he attacks, by preventing him from carrying the position held by the defensive troops. The position taken up is selected, as far as the mission will permit, with reference to its natural defensive features. Since the idea of offensive combat is absent, every advantage is taken of obstacles, natural or artificial, that hinder or altogether prevent the advance of the enemy. Negative rather than positive measures are relied upon to prevent the enemy from seizing the position. In this form of defense, the firing line is made as strong as possible from the first. If the flanks are not secured by other means, reserves strong enough for that purpose must be provided, but no reserves need be held for a decisive counter-attack. Supports and local reserves need be only strong enough to replace losses, to strengthen or reinforce the firing line where the enemy's attack is most threatening, and to repair breaches in the line.

F.S.R. 185. The purely passive defense is justified where the sole object of events is to gain time, or to hold certain positions pending the issue of events in other parts of the field. Its results, when it accomplishes its mission, can never be other than negative.

The Active Defense.

F.S.R. 186. The active defense or, the defense seeking a favorable decision, is the only form of defense that can secure positive results. A force whose intentions are offensive may at times be forced to assume the defensive either voluntarily in order to gain time or to secure some advantage over the enemy, or involuntarily, as where, in recontre, the enemy gets a start in deployment for action, or where the enemy's attack is impetuous and without sufficient preparation. In either case the defensive force contents itself from parrying the blows of the enemy, while gathering its strength and looking for the opening to strike a decisive blow.

F.S.R. 187. The crisis of this form of the defensive to the counter-attack, which marks the change from the defensive to the offensive. Upon the superior leader falls the responsibility of perceiving the right moment at which this change should be made and of having at hand the means necessary to effect it. The general reserve affords him the weapon necessary for his purpose. In this class of the defensive, therefore, strong supports and reserves are essential. The firing line is made as short as possible at first, in order to permit of the holding out of local supports and reserves strong enough to meet all movements of the enemy and to hold the line throughout up to the time of the decisive COUNTER-attack, and the retention until that time of a reserve strong enough to make a counter-attack a success. An open field of fire for effective and close ranges is essential. Obstacles immediately in front of the position that might impede the counter-attack are objectionable.

Defensive Positions and Intrenchments.

I.D.R. 489. The first requirement of a good position is a clear field of fire and view to the front and exposed flanks to a distance of 600 to 800 yards or more. The length of front should be suitable to the size of the command and the FLANKS should be secure. The position should have lateral communication and cover for supports and reserves. It should be one which the enemy can not avoid, but must attack or give up his mission. A position having all these advantages will rarely, if ever, be found. The one should be taken which conforms closest to the description.

I.D.R. 490. The natural cover of the position should be fully utilized. In addition, it should be strengthened by fieldworks and obstacles. The best protection is afforded by deep, narrow, inconspicuous trenches. If little time is available, as much as practicable must be done. That the fieldworks may not be needed should not cause their construction to be omitted, and the fact that they have been constructed should not influence the action of a commander, if conditions are found to be other than expected.

I.D.R. 491. When time and troops are available the preparations include the necessary communicating and cover trenches, head cover, bombproofs, etc. The fire trenches should be well supplied with ammunition. The supports are placed close at hand in cover trenches when natural cover is not available.

I.D.R. 492. dummy trenches frequently cause the hostile artillery to waste time and ammunition and to divert its fire.

Deployment for Defense.

I.D.R. 495. The density of the whole deployment depends upon the expected severity of the action, the character of the enemy, the condition of the flanks, the field of fire, the terrain, and the available artificial or natural protection for the troops.

I.D.R. 496. If exposed, the firing line should be as dense in defense as in attack. If the firing line is well intrenched and has a good field of fire, it may be made thinner. Weaker supports are permissible. For the same number of troops the front occupied on the defensive may therefore be longer than on the offensive, the battalions placing more companies in the firing line.

I.D.R. 497. If it is intended only to delay the enemy, a fairly strong deployment is sufficient, but if decisive results are desired, a change to the offensive must be contemplated and the corresponding strength in rear provided. This strength is in the reserve, which should be as large as the demands of the firing line and supports permit. Even in a passive defense the reserve should be as strong as in the attack, unless the flanks are protected by other means.

Use of Ground.

I.D.R. 406. The position of firers must afford a suitable field of fire. The ground should permit constant observation of the enemy, and yet enable the men to secure some cover when not actually firing. Troops whose target is for the moment hidden by unfavorable ground, either move forward to better ground or seek to execute cross fire on another target.

I.D.R. 407. The likelihood of a target being hit depends to a great extent upon its visibility. By skillful use of ground, a firing line may reduce its visibility without loss of fire power. Sky lines are particularly to be avoided.

Requisites of a Good Defensive Position.[69]

If you were looking for a good defensive position, what points would you have in mind and of these points, which would be the most important? The requisites to be sought in a good defensive position are:

1. A clear field of fire up to the effective range of the artillery.

2. flanks that are naturally secure or that can be made so by the use of the reserves.

3. Extent of ground suitable to the strength of the force to occupy it.

4. Effective cover and concealment for the troops, especially reserves.

5. Good communications throughout the position.

6. Good lines of retreat.

All of these advantages will seldom if ever be found in the position selected. The one should be taken which conforms closest to the description, but you should bear in mind that a good field of fire and effective cover, in the order named, are the most important requisites. In tracing the lines for the trenches, avoid salient (a hill, spur, woods, etc., that juts out from the general line in the direction of the enemy). Avoid placing the fire trench on the skyline. Locate it on or below the military crest (the crest from which you can see all of the ground in the front and are not silhouetted against the horizon).

---

[69] *P.M.*, 250.

Preparing a Defensive Position.[70]

Now let us suppose ourselves as part of a battalion that is to occupy a defensive position. What would probably be done? How and in what order would it be done? What would the major do? He would decide upon the kind of defense (active or passive) to offer, and then find a suitable defensive position in harmony with his plans. He would determine exactly where the firing and other trenches are to be dug. He would then call up the company commanders and issue his defense order in which the task of each company would be made clear. Those to occupy the firing line would be assigned a sector of ground to the front to defend and a corresponding section of the fire trench to construct. The supports would construct their trenches and the communicating trenches. He would, if necessary, issue the necessary orders to protect the front and flanks by sending out patrols. He would indicate how the position is to be strengthened and make arrangements for distributing the extra ammunition. If time is a serious consideration, the major would direct the work to be done in the order of its importance, which is ordinarily as follows:

1. Clearing of foreground to improve the field of fire and construction of fire trench.

2. Head or overhead cover concealment.

3. Placing obstacles and recording images.

4. Cover trenches for supports and local reserves.

5. Communicating trenches.

6. Widening and deepening of trench; interior conveniences.

Now having cleared the foreground, dug the trenches, recorded ranges to the important objects in each sector, etc., the position can be occupied. The citizen ordinarily pictures the firing trench full of soldiers when he is told the trenches are occupied. Not so. Patrols will be operating well to the front to give timely warning to one or two sentinels in each company fire trench of the approach of

---

[70] *P.M.*, 251.

the enemy. These sentinels would in turn inform the company which would probably be resting in the trenches to the rear.

Clearly, this particular defense in Bois d'Ogons was a "passive" one: "*F.S.R.* 185. The purely passive defense is justified where the sole object of events is to gain time, or to hold certain positions pending the issue of events in other parts of the field. Its results, when it accomplishes its mission, can never be other than negative." The other tenets of defense though, such as depth, or fields of fire, etc., cannot always be exploited simply because of your position in the line. Sometimes your unit will be assigned a position that is just a bad place to defend. But don't worry, as it's probably a bad place to attack, too! For us, we put as many supporting weapons up front, guarded our flanks with patrols, and kept a substantial reserve, no less than a platoon. Army Regulations warned us about deploying our reserves in "driblets." In fact, maintaining a reserve in the defense is far more important than holding a strong front line. As a rule of thumb, go in thirds: one-third of your command should be held in reserve. If the enemy breaks through, then commit the entire reserve—throw back the enemy—and return said unit back to mobile reserve status.

The other thing to remember about defending at night is not to fire the supporting weapons like M.G.s or A.R.s first (if at all). Instead, throw a hand grenade, as it won't give away your position. Also, as stated in Army Regulations and proven in battle by our experience, be prepared to use the bayonet during periods of limited visibility.

For M.G.s in the defense, particular attention must be paid to the necessity for sweeping all ravines and valleys with enfilading fire. A.R.s like Chauchats, Lewis Guns, or, later, Browning Automatic Rifles (B.A.R.s) should cover areas not covered by the M.G.s. It is also expected that each pointer or gun commander calculates the necessary firing data, provides limiting stakes and flash arresters (if available—to conceal bursts at night), creates a range card (a terrain sketch with T & E coordinates), and familiarizes himself with the routes of approach to all other M.G. positions, front or rear, which it may become necessary for his crew to occupy. He should also know the locations and the fields of fire of his own and neighboring M.G.s. Furthermore, all pointers are expected to turn over to relieving units all available data which will be necessary for the proper functioning of the crew.

At 8:45 P.M., Maj. Montague reported to Col. Worrilow: "HALIBUT has reached objective and is digging in." We in the 1/318 (Red Squares) obtained similar results as we were able to reach the northwestern edge of Bois de Fays once we took out several Hun M.G. positions along our axis of advance in the same fashion, losing a few men per each Hun gun taken. I don't remember who we lost during this phase. I do remember, however, that once we reached the tree line that fronted the Madeleine Farm, looking west, we too were driven further back into the woods by concentrated German artillery and M.G. fire that was being directed from *KRIEMHILDE*.

By the close of Oct. 5 therefore, the 80th Division had finally secured Bois d'Ogons after suffering some 2,000 casualties. And for the rest of that hellish night in Bois d'Ogons and Fays, we once again suffered frequent artillery and gas attacks, forcing us to wear our hated masks almost all the time, even as we attempted to sleep. It was either that or die. For his actions on Oct. 4-5, Lt. Col. Charles Keller, the new commanding officer of the 317th Infantry, was awarded the D.S.M. His citation reads:

> *He took command of a regiment at a critical moment, after two unsuccessful assaults had been made by the brigade. He reorganized the regiment under fire and made possible the taking and holding of Bois d'Ogons, displaying the highest order of leadership and exhibiting the masterful qualities of a commander.* [71]

Two other soldiers from the 317th Infantry were also cited for heroism while operating in Bois d'Ogons during this period. They are representative of the thousands of gallant actions that were performed that memorable day. The noted soldiers are: Sergeant Manley Bradley of Company D and Sergeant James T. Jenkins of Company G. Their citations read:

> *Sergeant Bradley was wounded in the head while leading his platoon across a valley swept by machine gun fire but he continued to lead his men to their objective, refusing to report to the dressing station until he was ordered to do so.*

> *Patrolling himself in front of the line, Sergeant Jenkins came upon a M.G. emplacement manned by a German officer and three men. He wounded the*

---

[71] As cited in *317th Infantry*, 89.

officer and one soldier by rifle fire, captured the other two men and took them with the M.G. to the rear. [72]

October 6, 1918.

Weather: Clear.

Roads: Fair.

Sometime around 2:00 A.M., Sunday, Oct. 6, 1918, we in 1/318th Infantry were relieved by a battalion from the Ivy Division and were ordered to a march to Dannevoux and await further orders. For the rest of the day, the bulk of Jamerson's 159th Inf. Brig. remained in defensive positions in Bois d'Ogons, with sections from the 313th M.G. Battalion providing primary defensive fires. At around noon, 2/319 and 2/317 moved about four hundred yards back through the woods to enable the "big guns" of Goodfellow's 315th Artillery to reduce enemy positions just north of *Ferme Madeleine*. This artillery fire was timed to support an attack by the 3rd Division on our left. After completion of the barrage, which ended at about 3:00 P.M., 2/319 and 2/317 returned to their tree-line defensive positions. During the day's operations, Lt. Charles K. Dillingham, M/3/318 Infantry, the regiment's designated support battalion, was later awarded the Army's Distinguished Service Cross. His citation reads:

> *For extraordinary heroism in action near NANTILLOIS, France, 6 October, 1918. Lieutenant Dillingham, on duty as battalion intelligence officer, twice volunteered and led a patrol through woods known to be occupied by hostile machine guns. Working his way through artillery and machine gun fire, he succeeded in ascertaining the position of units on the right and left of his own. Throughout the action around NANTILLOIS and the BOIS DE OGONS this officer was a constant inspiration to his men by his devotion to duty and disregard for personal safety.* [73]

---

[72] *Ibid.*, 90.

[73] As cited in *318th Infantry*, 69.

Throughout the rest of the day, batteries from Heiner's artillery brigade fired several harassing, raking, or zone searching missions along *KRIEMHILDE*. It also suffered some casualties. For example, Gun 3 of B/1/313th Artillery burst and acting Corporal Thomas S. Riley from Weston, West Virginia, was killed near Bois Brieulles. He was the first man in 313th Artillery to be killed outright. Several others were horribly wounded and were carried on stretchers along the road that led back to Septsarges until an ambulance was found. According to Lt. Crowell of the 313th Artillery: "The trip was made under gas and shell fire, the men at times having to wear their masks."[74] Lt. John B. Wise of the 314th Artillery was wounded by "bursting shell" and was also evacuated to the aid station.

As Jamerson's shot-up 159th Inf. Brig. held its positions in Bois d'Ogons, Cronkhite ordered Brett's 160th Inf. Brig. to relieve it in place, no later than dawn, Oct. 8, minus the divisional M.G. battalions, which were to stay in place, anchoring the defensive line. Maj. Ashby Williams of 1/320th Infantry remembered his moving into the front lines around Nantillois during the early-morning hours of Oct. 7:

> *I started out with my company commanders and my orderly, toward Nantillois. We followed for the most part the little trench railway that wound around the barren ridges until we reached the Nantillois-Septsarges Road at a pint about 500 yards from Nantillois. There were many evidences that a great struggle had taken place over this ground in the battle of a few days before. Equipment and broken wagons and dead horses were everywhere. There were no dead men scattered over the fields, as they had been picked up and laid in a long row on the bank beside the road leading to Nantillois. There were perhaps a hundred of them. It was indeed a pathetic sight. They were Boche and Americans, lying side-by-side, calm and peaceful and unhating in death waiting for that final act of the crude hands of the living to shove them into the waiting grave, back into the bosom of the mother from which they sprang, to be known and seen no more upon the face of the earth... [I met with Col. Love, commander of the 319th Infantry, in an abandoned German bunker.] We went over the entire situation together, he explaining to me for the first time that my battalion would likely take over a sector in the front line, running through Bois d'Ogons. Col. Love was frankly not optimistic about the situation at the front and did not hesitate to*

---

[74] As cited in *313th Artillery*, 52.

picture to me the great difficulties I might be expected to encounter. He was undoubtedly impressed with the fact that former attempts to advance beyond the place had been attended with such sanguinary results.[75]

Lt. Edward Lukens of 3/320th Infantry similarly remembered:

Maj. Emory led the way, for which I admired him, for this was not to be a fight, but an ordinary digging job that he might easily have delegated to a junior officer had he been less conscientious. After a hard struggle through the mud across and open field, we came to a road near Nantillois, and it was on the brow of the hill in front of the road that the trenches had been taped out by the engineers. For over three hours the men dug, in darkness, rain and constant apprehension of shelling, until the early-morning hours the job was declared done, tools turned in, and we started back to where our packs were piled.[76]

Jamerson's 159th Inf. Brig. had had a rough time of it and was persistently dogged by ill-fortune—primarily due to the situation it was emplaced. In attacking Bois d'Ogons as it did, defended by a very adept enemy, it did not have the benefit of hours of corps and army artillery shellacking, of fresh troops, or of adequate accurate information. Yet we had pushed forward two km on a two-km front. Up to this point, Keller's 317th Infantry had lost 92 K.I.A. and 433 W.I.A., a total of 525, including the casualties while serving with Brett's 160th Inf. Brig. My very own 318th Infantry had suffered 941 casualties, including 107 K.I.A., 832 W.I.A., and 2 M.I.A. Of these, 34 were killed and 153 were wounded while serving with the 4th Division. All told, our losses were about a third of our strength. In 2/318, whose casualties were highest in the division, four officers and 46 E.M. lost their lives and the wounded totaled nine officers and 291 E.M. These figures do not include the rather severe casualties of Maj. Montague's 2/319 or Maj. Huidekopper's 313th M.G. Battalion.

Many recommendations were made for the D.S.C. for actions performed in Bois d'Ogons. But "because of the lack of definite knowledge of how to property submit these recommendations, very few of them were approved."[77] We never did buy this line, but that was Worrilow's explanation to us. There is no doubt that it does matter who the commanding officer

---

[75] As cited in *1/320th Infantry*, 107.

[76] As cited in *3/320th Infantry*, 80.

[77] *318th Infantry*, 69.

is. Some simply think that an infantryman's job is to be brave and that "above and beyond" is to be truly super human. Others, however, saw "above and beyond" as compared to someone at home, working on a farm or in a factory. In truth, somewhere in the middle is probably the best place for a commander to be when it comes to awards. The other factor to consider is that once an "extraordinarily heroic act" is performed, it must be witnessed, those witnesses need to have survived to report it, and they had to actually like or respect the recipient. That, plus the officers had to recover from the shock they themselves suffered to even write them up. Nevertheless, the 318th Infantry Regiment takes just pride that several soldiers actually received said decoration.

318th Infantry Regiment, 80th (Blue Ridge) Division Casualties.

Sept. 26-Oct. 6. 1918.

Unit	K.I.A. Officers	K.I.A. Men	W.I.A. Officers	W.I.A. Men	M.I.A Officers	M.I.A Men
H.Q.	0	5	0	49	0	0
M.G.	0	3	2	40	0	0
Supply	0	0	0	3	0	0
Medical	0	2	3	8	0	0
1/318	3	30	8	242	0	2
2/318	4	46	7	291	0	0
3/318	0	15	5	174	0	0
Total	7	101	25	807	0	2

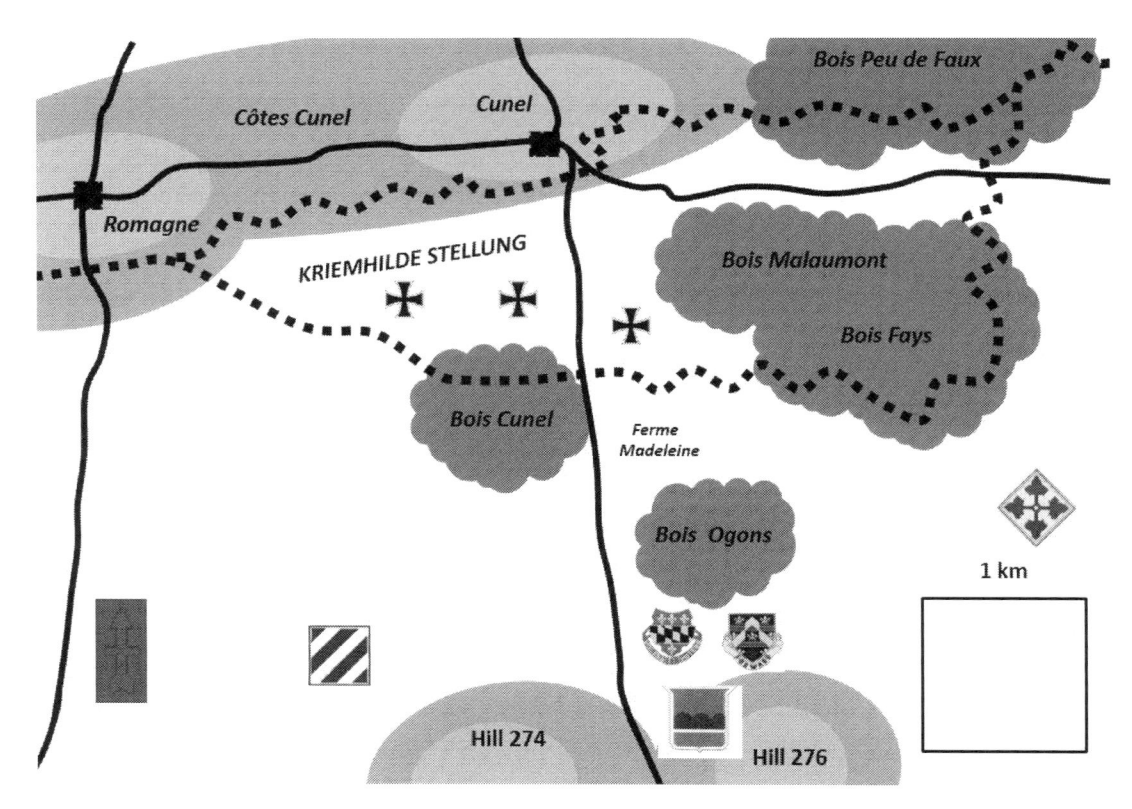

160th Inf. Brig., 80th Division Area of Operations, Oct. 7-8, 1918. The 320th Inf. is on the right and the 319th Inf. is on the left. The mission: demonstrate in the vicinity of *Ferme Madeleine* while the 3rd and 4th Infantry Divisions conducted a double-envelopment, breaching *KRIEMHILDE* and taking Cunel.

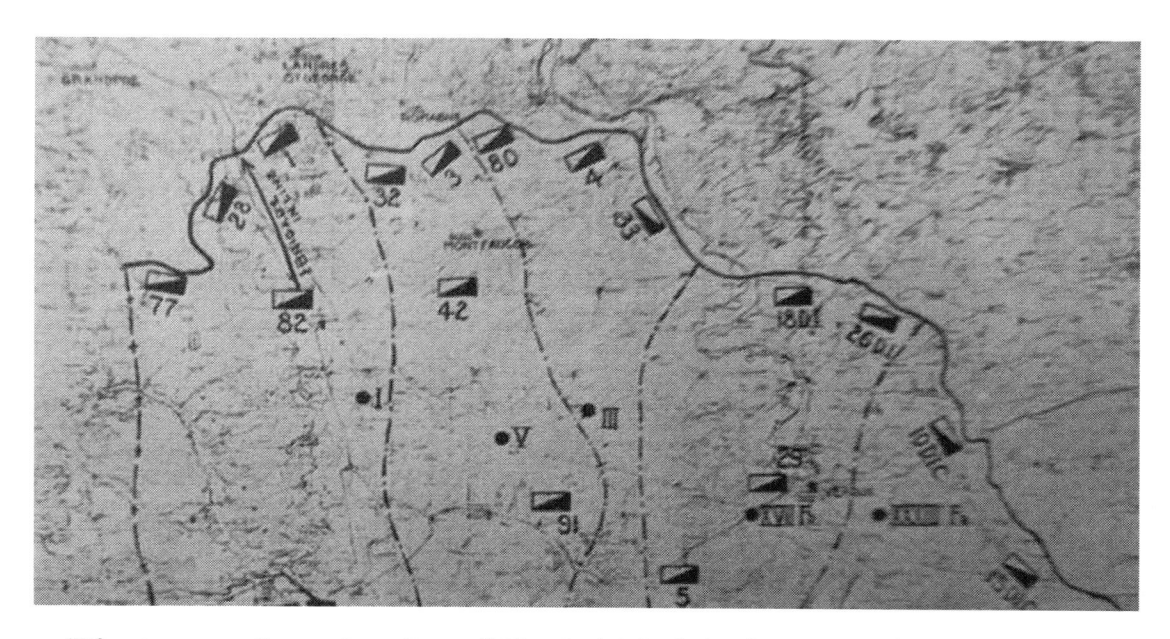

"The Argonne Operation, Oct. 7." The 80th Div. is in the center of the attack. This is a period map.

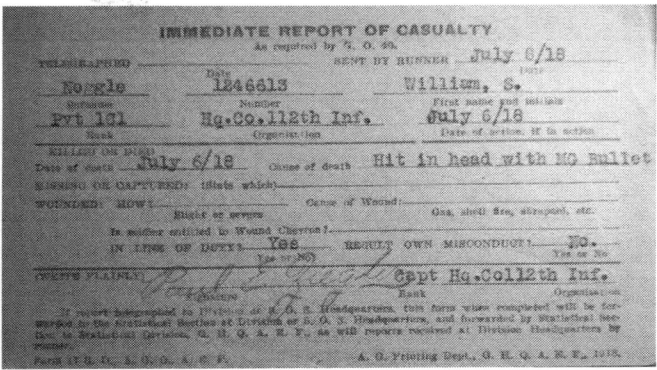

One of our supply camions being used as an ambulance (L) and a copy of "Immediate report of Casualty" (R). This states that Pvt. Wm. S. Noggle, Service No. 1246613 of H.Q./112th Inf. was K.I.A. "Hit in head with MG Bullet" on July 8, 1918.

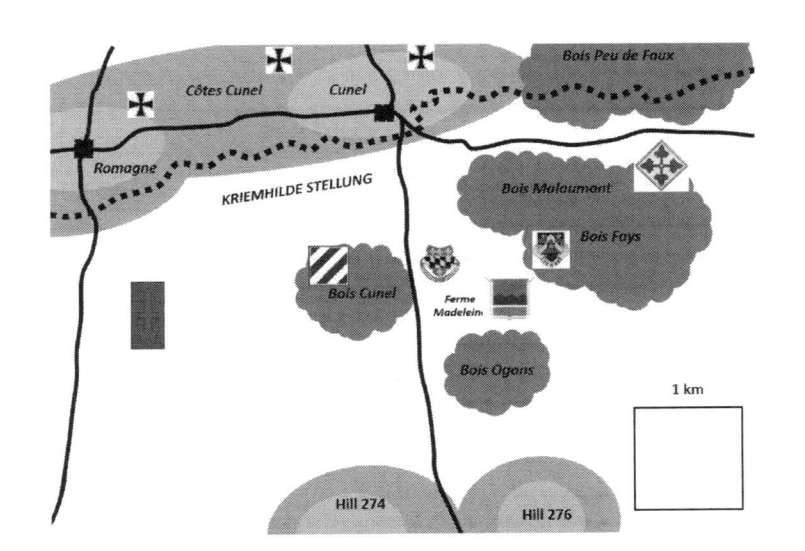

160th Inf. Brig., 80th Division Area of Operations, Oct. 9-11, 1918. The Hun fought ferociously to maintain *KRIEMHILDE*.

Scene on the left captures the combat around *Ferme Madeleine* and a typical Hun M.G. position along the Heights of Cunel, facing south (R). We had to push through their blasted beaten zones (middle of pic.) and get into their defilade to have any chance of moving forward. And the 80th Division Always Moves Forward!

We can't make it any more clear than this: the LARGEST AMERICAN CEMETERY IN FRANCE was built between Cunel and Romagne. This was the area that the 3rd, 4th, and 80th Divisions fought, scraped, clawed, and bled. R.I.P.

"Supply Train Passing Through Cuisy, Oct. 11, 1918" (L) and Y.M.C.A. Hut at Les Islettes Petites (R).

A real shower and new uniform thanks to the Q.M. Corps! It helped clean "the animal" off us at Les Islettes Petites.

The inventor John Browning's son, Lt. Val Browning, with the M1917 Browning Auto Rifle (B.A.R.) (L) and "Soldier with a Browning M1917 Automatic Rifle, 30.06." (R). We actually had Lt. Browning demonstrate his wares to us. We so loved the B.A.R. that we thought that every Dough should have one!

Lt. Val Browning himself demonstrated the new M1917 M.G. to M.G.ers of the Blue Ridge Division. It fed better and faster than the older M1915.

The popular Maj. Gen. Joseph Dickman (L), commander of the 3rd Inf. Div., the I Corps, and the Third U.S. Army in France. The 80th Division was attached to Dickman's I Corps for our Third and Final Push up the Meuse-Argonne. Generals John Pershing and Charles Summerall (R). Summerall, on the right, commanded the the V Corps upon the relief of General Cameron.

151

The Kaiser's last Army Chief of Staff, Wilhelm Groener with his wife (L) and Crown Prince Max von Baden (R), the man who helped facilitate the armistice. The prince is mourning the death of the Second German Empire with his black arm band.

"At home in a shell hole, 10-24-18" with the 319th Inf. in the Argonne Forest (L) and "Fôret d'Argonne. The Germans were turned back at this point" (R).

The intrepid Maj. Sweeney, 1/318th Inf. at the battalion P.C. in the Argonne Forest (L) and a French *camion* (motor truck) driven by French Indo-Chinese (R).

Chapter 3

The Battle for *Ferme Madeleine* and Recovery (Oct. 7-31, 1918).

October 7, 1918.

Weather: Fair.

Roads: Good.

During the morning of Oct. 7, Brett's 160th Inf. Brig. completed its relief of Jamerson's shot-up 159th Brigade in Bois d'Ogons. We later learned that Jamerson's brigade had been up against "the best in the German Army," which was desperate to stop our advance through Bois d'Ogons, *viz.*, elements from the 5th Bavarian Reserve Division, the Prussian 28th (Flying Shock) Division, and the Prussian 115th and 236th Infantry Divisions, as well as several *Sturm* or *Stoss* battalions.[78] Maj. Ashby Williams, leading his 1/320 into the new position, proceeded north through Nantillois in an effort to obtain more guides than the two sent by Col. Love. With him went the battalion surgeon, adjutant, intelligence men and runners. He wrote:

> *I raised a great deal of fuss and even went so far as to cuss a little, as I considered that I should have one guide for each company at least, even one for each platoon. My troops were going in the darkness into an area which neither I nor my officers had reconnoitered in daylight... We were grateful for the darkness that gave a sense of security from the whining shells that searched the area, and the noise of many guns with their flashes lighting the sky stimulated and exhilarated the body and mind beyond all powers of description. I remember how fatigued in mind and body we were after the four-kilometer hike and how relieved we were when we finally, about 1:00 o'clock of the morning of October 8, reached Col. Love's headquarters and went inside to place of safety. When we went through the front room of the vault I had to literally walk over the top of the men who were lying on the floor, so crowded were they, and the atmosphere was so tense that it could have been cut with a knife... I remember as we got into the colonel's room a circumstance which under different environment might have been laughable, but betrayed the state of mind of the men in that room. The vault was closed up tight with heavy iron blinds, and the*

---

[78] *317th Infantry*, 67 and *319th Infantry*, 31.

candles were burning all around the room. My doctor had rolled a cigarette and he struck a match to light it. Col. Love turned on him in an instant and said: "For God's sake, man, put out that light. Do you want us all killed in here?" [We then continued our advance north]. The march of my troops up the hill [into Bois d'Ogons] that night was all Col. Love told me it would be. It was hell. The night was dark and the way was difficult and the Boche were sweeping the place from across the Meuse with light and heavy shells and with those most dreaded demons of all weapons, the Austrian 88s, or the "Whizbangs" as they are called. He was also putting over gas in great quantities. Indeed, it is hard to understand how any living creature could have passed up that hill that night without injury, and it seems almost incredible that we should have suffered only fourteen casualties... My P. C. was on a ridge about 600 meters north of Nantillois... It was a little oblong affair, perhaps four feet high in the front, about five feet wide and ten feet long, built up about a foot above the surface of the ground and covered with timber and earth. It resembled, indeed, a sunken log cabin, with... its dirt walls, and dirt floor, and shelter-half before the entrance to keep the candle light from shining out toward the Boche, as he had built the place and the opening was, of course, in his direction.[79]

Brig. Gen. George H. Jamerson, commander of the 159th Inf. Brig., 80th Division.

Brig. Gen. Lloyd M. Brett, commander of the 160th Inf. Brig., 80th Division.

In his "Post Operation Report" about our hellish time in Bois d'Ogons, Brig. Gen. Jamerson wrote a scathing review.[80] It reads, in part:

---

[79] As cited in *1/320*, 110.

[80] As cited in Stultz, 446.

> 1. Orders for Corps attack on 4 October 1918 were not issued in time to permit proper reconnaissance or instruction of subordinate commanders.
>
> 2. Our casualties from flanking M.G. fire and violent artillery fire from the front and right flank were severe.
>
> 3. It was demonstrated during the action of 3-6 October that a position defended by belts of flanking machine gun fire can only be successfully attacked when absolutely coordinated and effective liaison with neighboring troops is maintained at all times.
>
> 4. The fact that incorrect information was received as to the positions reached by neighboring troops was responsible for much misunderstanding and heavy losses from flanking M.G. fire from points which were reported to be in our hands.
>
> 5. The scarcity of maps available during these operations was a decided handicap.
>
> 6. On 4 October, north of Nantillois, an Infantry contact plane called for our front line. At that time our front line was under flanking M.G. fire and in such a position that to have displayed panels as desired by the plane would have involved heavy casualties. In addition there were low-flying enemy planes about and a display of panels would have disclosed our exact line to the enemy, with the probability that our front would have suffered still more heavily from the enemy's fire.

We found that too many officers above the rank of captain (i.e., field and general grades) too often got too touchy when it came to constructive criticism from subordinates. On the one hand, we were expected to follow orders without question. On the other, as explained by Baron von Steuben, American soldiers also expect to be told "why" and not to be treated like simple automations. We were taught to tell the truth—to "tell it how it is." Sometimes, if a field or general grade officer sensed "disloyalty" or "lack of enthusaiam" or "quibbling" from a subordinate officer, however, too many them removed said officer and said officer ended up in a dead-end position. In war, I'm not so sure that this is the best policy, but it's the way our Army operates. I guess my only suggestion to an officer who needs to constructively criticize an operation is to "make it about the plan, and not the man." Don't personalize things. Say things like, "we need to do a better job at…" In war, when nerves are fried and life is cheap, this is very hard to do. But do it! Get another officer to help you write it. Ask the other officer to "filter" what you say and to "focus on the plan and not the man." Cronkhite, in his operations report, backed Jamerson's assertions, which fell squarely on the lap of the corps commander, General Bullard:

> *The entire operation of the 159th Brigade was seriously hampered by misinformation coming from the flanking divisions. As an example of this, at 9 o'clock on the morning of the 4th, the 3rd Division on our left reported that it had reached the Trench 9245 and the 4th Division on our right reported that it had reached well within the Bois de Fays. This information was communicated to the III Corps and by them given to this division. Acting on this information, repeated attempts were made to outflank the strongly held Bois des Ogons. However, in every case heavy machine gun fire was encountered, and it was later learned that neither of the flanking divisions had advanced their line as far as our own.*[81]

By mid-day, the 319th Infantry was on the left and the 320th Infantry was on the right, with two companies up and two in back. They were told that they were going to attack across the Ferme Madeleine and straight into the concrete-reinforced German M.G. nests atop Côtes Cunel and *KRIEMHILDE*. Capt. Charles R. Herr of F/2/319th Infantry remembers:

> *Throughout the day the Boche shelled us heavily; his aeroplanes were constantly overhead correcting the fire of his artillery. Out-posts were established and every effort made to make the position capable of defense. The snipers came up from the rear with orders to ascertain the strength of the*

---

[81] As cited in Stultz, 447.

enemy. They had no sooner gotten beyond our line than the enemy cut loose with M.G. and artillery fire.[82]

The batteries of the 313th and 314th Artillery also suffered intermittent German artillery fire throughout the day, with "considerable amounts of gas being used." 2/314th Artillery, for example, lost Maj. Granville Fortesue, Capt. Dwight Beebe, Capt. Samuel B. Ridge (the Battalion Surgeon), Lt. Frank Heacock, and five E.M. to gas attacks. A Hun artillery observation balloon from the Heights of the Meuse looked down upon our batteries around Hill 295 and directed several counter-battery fire missions against them. *Les Boche* even hurled massive 210mm *Minenwerfer* bombs into Bois Septsarges, killing several S.O.S. men from the 80th and 4th Infantry Divisions. The other problem was that scores of German aircraft, who seemingly owned the skies, continued to swarm the line, spraying it with M.G. fire. They would also spot our artillery, run circles around them, and pop flares, alerting their own artillery crews.[83]

This artillery fire kept the signalmen busy, as telephone lines, which were insulated with cloth, constantly went down. Telephone lines from the O.P.s to the gun line, lines from the batteries to the battalions, lines from the battalions back to brigade were constantly cut. Personnel from Whitaker's 305th Ammunition Battalion were also kept quite busy trying to keep the hungry guns fed. Every night, like clockwork, they had to drive their caissons back to the corps ammunition dumps in Cuisy, which was a "hot and happenin' place." The roads there were under constant enemy shellfire. The decrease of horse power among the artillery battalions was only getting worse, especially once influenza started to take hold and the horses were forced to work beyond their limits, like the men.[84] According to Capt. Peck of the 319th Infantry:

Throughout the night of Oct. 7-8, the shellfire was particularly heavy over the area, a continuous fire of H.E. and gas being directed at the crossroads in Nantillois and the batteries located in close-proximity to it. A number of casualties were suffered in the village during the night and runners from the H.Q. and the medical detachment being constantly exposed to the fire. The regimental aid station was located in the cellar of a ruined building near the

---

[82] As cited in *2/319th Infantry*, 11.

[83] *314th Artillery*, 40.

[84] *313th Artillery*, 53.

water point miraculously escaped that night, but was hit later, two or three men—one medical officer—being killed and others wounded.[85]

Maj. Ashby Williams of 1/320th Infantry similarly remembered:

It was hell. The night was dark and the way difficult and the Boche was sweeping the place from across the Meuse with light and heavy shells and with those most dreaded demons of all weapons, the Austrian 88s, or the whiz-bangs, as they were called. Indeed, it is hard to understand how any living creature could have [survived in the position we held that night].[86]

Following its relief by Love's 319th Infantry, Worrilow's 318th Infantry reached the designated concentration area southeast of Cuisy mentally and physically exhausted, and, due to numerous casualties among its officers and N.C.O.s, rather badly organized. From Sept. 26-Oct. 6, one must remember that we had been under constant enemy fire and had suffered numerous casualties on an hourly basis. The other infantry regiments of the division shared a similar, if not even worse, fate. Lt. Edward Lukens of the 320th Infantry put it succinctly when he wrote: "There were more divisions used and more companies and battalions used up, in the neighborhood of the little village of Cunel, than any other place that I know of on the American front, and the [80th Division], many another good outfit, had its turn on these hills, gained a little ground, and went back for replacements."[87] Let it be remembered that the main American Military Cemetery in France is built atop the Heights of Cunel. That, in and of itself, speaks volumes.

As Jamerson's 160th Inf. Brig. assumed their new positions Up the Line, Bullard issued orders for the next corps attack. Here they are, truncated for clarity, as well as the converted operational memo cut by division H.Q.:[88]

---

[85] As cited in *319th Infantry*, 31.

[86] As cited in *1/320th Infantry*, 109.

[87] As cited in *3/320th Infantry*, 78.

[88] As cited in Stultz, 457-59.

1-2

From: Chief of Staff.
To: Commanding General, 160th Infantry Brigade.
Subject: Operations.

1. I am enclosing herewith copies of field order No. 24, 3rd Corps.

2. The Commanding General directs that you hold your entire brigade (less Montague's battalion 319th Infantry) in readiness to execute the provisions of this order and especially to carry out the last sentence of paragraph 3 (b), (c) of it. Authority will be obtained by these headquarters for the use of the 320th Infantry now bivouacked south of the Cuisy-Montfaucon Road. Should necessity arise for the use of these troops in the execution of Field Order 24 prior to the receipt of the authority referred to above, you will be authorized to use them upon application to these headquarters.

3. Artillery: The Commanding General, 155th Artillery Brigade will see you and Colonel Welsh, at which conference you will arrange:

(a) The line on which the barrage will be put down.

(b) How long it will remain stationary.

(c) The rate at which it will roll, which will be not faster than 100 meters in 8 minutes unless ordered by higher authority.

(d) The distance to the front that the barrage will advance.

(e) The plans for bombarding with the 155s of the fringes of the woods in the Divisional Sector.

(f) The plans for the use of smoke barrages.

(g) Plans for the utilization of the Gas and Flame Company under your command. This organization is equipped with 4" Stokes Mortars, and have a range of 1100 yds. and fire thermite projectiles.

2-2

4. Infantry: Special measures will be taken for the advance of the infantry:

(a) To insure their starting at the proper time and following the barrage closely.

(b) To employ thin lines of scouts to work around machine gun nests and attack them from the flanks and rear.

(c) To mop up the ground passed over.

(d) To employ the least vulnerable formations and take the fullest advantage of any available cover in passing over the ground lying between Nantillois and the south edge of the Bois des Ogons which is exposed to artillery fire from the N.E.

(e) To echelon the battalions in depth during the attack and prevent troops from crowding into the forward line.

(f) To provide for the protection of the left flank of the attacking line against M.G. fire from the Bois de Cunel.

5. Liaison: Special precautions will be taken to maintain liaison throughout the command and with these headquarters. Troops of the forward line will be especially instructed to stake out their line with the panels when called for by aeroplane.

6. All men will carry two extra bandoliers of ammunition and an effort will be made to provide a supply of phosphorus hand grenades. C-1 will take up this matter with the least practicable delay.

7. All of the details for this operation to be made with the least practicable delay so that it can be launched on receipt of orders to do so. Liaison with the troops of the 4th Division on the right and the 3rd Division on the left will be maintained so that the closest cooperation may be secured with them.

By command of Major General Cronkhite:
J. B. Barnes,
Lieut. Colonel, General Staff,
For the Chief of Staff.

```
                          P. C. III Army Corps, A.E.F.
7 October 1918.
17:30 o'clock.
                    S E C R E T.

Field Order No. 24.
Maps: Same as Field Order No. 23.
```

1. No change in the hostile situation. The 1st American Army will seize and hold the COTES de MEUSE east of CONSENVOYE on October 8, 1918, and on the following day the heights west of ROMAGNE-sous-MONTFAUCON.

2. The Third Corps will protect the flanks of the attack of the V Corps and XVIII Corps.

3. (b) The 4th Division and 80th Division will accurately establish their own and enemy front lines and prepare complete rolling barrage tables for their front. They will prepare complete plans for bombarding with 155s the fringes of woods in their sectors as far as the Combined Army First Phase Line. Plans will also be prepared for the use of smoke screens to the extent possible with the means at their disposal. They will be prepared to attack and seize the heights in their immediate front upon orders from the Corps Commander....
(d) The 5th Division will be prepared to march on two hours' notice.
(e) ARTILLERY: The Corps and Divisional artillery will assist the attack of the V and XVII Corps by counter battery and interdiction fire as opportunities offer; also be prepared to support the prospective attack of the III Corps.
(f) The Air Service will carry out its mission in accordance with Field Order No. 23 and be prepared for an attack by this Corps....
(g) DIVISION COMMANDERS WILL TAKE SPECIAL MEASURES TO INSURE THE INFANTRY FOLLOWING CLOSELY THE BARRAGE.

4. Administrative details: No change.

5. P. C.s and Axes of Liaison: No change.

```
                    By command of Major Brig. Gen.  BULLARD:
                                    A. W. BJORNSTAD,
                                 Brigadier Brig. Gen. , G. S.,
                                         Chief of Staff.
```

A simple perusal of the above orders/instructions will show how we became more and more reliant upon smoke and bombs. The comment: "To employ thin lines of scouts to work around M.G. nests and attack them from the flanks and rear" was inferred from the regulations and drawn from our post-operation reports. Although it's not a bad idea to publish "tactical recommendations" for subordinate units to follow, to enshrine them in an order to expect them to be followed at all times is somewhat whimsical if not impractical and wrong, in my opinion. But this is what higher command gives us: as much support as it can, coordination, and a view of the "bigger picture." Other than that, it's pretty much up to the company commanders, platoon leaders, top sergeants, platoon guides, squad leaders, and the men themselves to accomplish the mission.

Scary but true.

Typical "bivi" while on the move in France. Getz and I as well as all of the other Doughs were just trying to survive into the next day. On the right is an example how we used "pig tail" barb wire posts to help construct our bivis. This is one part of Army life we will not miss.

October 8, 1918.

Weather: Fair.

Roads: Good.

During the early-morning hours of Oct. 8, as units from Brett's 160th Inf. Brig. prepared for the up-and-coming *Götterdämmerung* against KRIEMHILDE at *Ferme Madeleine*, its men had to endure "severe gas shelling with a liberal mix of H.E," forcing them to wear their nose-pinching masks most of the night.[89] Capt. Peck of the 319th Infantry remembered:

> *The line remained at a standstill, the enemy maintaining an uninterrupted fire. During the night, the area was subjected to severe gas shelling with a liberal mixture of H.E. The concentration was so heavy in the valleys as to necessitate the wearing of masks most of the night. The personnel at regimental H.Q. wore their masks the greater part of the night, the runners and signalmen who were obliged to go and come in the darkness suffering fearfully. The runners were oftentimes the only means of communication, the buzzer line being put out of commission, many times daily, by shell fire.*[90]

Our own 155th Arty. Brig. of course answered in kind and the 313th Artillery gassed Hun positions in *Village Brieulles*, which was ablaze at this point. Lt. Crowell, the Telephone Officer of 313th Artillery wrote:

> *Brieulles enfiladed our infantry positions. The 4th Division had found it impracticable to take the town by storm as it would be gradually surrounded with the breaking of the Kriemhilde Stellung to the west. Our fire upon Brieulles was at a rate of three mustard shells and one H.E. after five minutes of preliminary lethal. Reports from the infantry indicated that this fire was very effective.*[91]

---

[89] *Götterdämmerung* is pronounced "Got-ter-dame-air-unk"; it is the mythological last battle of the gods—the end of the earth.

[90] *319th Infantry*, 32.

[91] As cited in *313th Artillery*, 52.

Maj. Ashby Williams, the commander of 1/320th Infantry, remembered the absolute devastation of the area—the real effects of modern warfare on the land and the people:

After daylight I received word from Col. Love that I would be held responsible for the safety of the forward zone. I determined, therefore, to go over the positions of the entire sector. [Bois d'Ogons], which is situated upon a crest, was literally torn to pieces with shells, great trees broken off and torn up by the roots, and the whole place saturated with the nauseating odor of phosgene gas. Capt. Sabiston, my orderly, and I started out, therefore, on the morning of Oct. 8 on our tour of inspection. By the light of day we could see what havoc had been wrought on the Americans in the attempts that had been made to advance beyond the Bois d'Ogons. Due to the continued heavy fire, details had not been able to police up the battle field, and dead men were scattered everywhere; some of them were my men who had been lost the night before, but most of them belonged to the battalions that had experienced such sanguinary results in their attempts to take the place. It was, indeed, a pathetic sight. We passed by Company D in the third echelon and on to Companies B and C that were in the trenches newly-constructed before the Bois d'Ogons in anticipation of a great drive, and thence on to the Bois d'Ogons. I stopped and talked with Capt. Hooper of the 319th Infantry, the fighting parson of Culpeper, Virginia, whose regiment occupied a sector on my left. After smoking a few of his cigarettes I went up the road further into the woods and came up to Capt. Ted Davant, whose M.G. company had been attached to my command for the operation. I passed along the wood road leading eastward to Company A and to the outpost line of that company along the north and northeast edge of the Bois d'Ogons. From the positions of the outpost lines I could see the Bois de Fays and the terrain to the front. I have often wondered why we were not shot to pieces as we were in plain view and range of the M.G.s we afterwards encountered. With the changes I made I considered the place will-nigh impregnable against any attack the Boche might put over.[92]

Soon after dawn, Brett's 160th Inf. brig. attacked north. As the day progressed, reconnaissance patrols from the 319th and 320th Infantry located several strong Hun M.G.

---

[92] As cited in *1/320*, 110.

positions in Bois Malaumont and Cunel and they were turned into targets for Heiner's 155th Arty. Brig.[93] While the big guns of the 315th Artillery were usually focused on counter-battery missions well-behind the front lines, they were also, according to doctrine and practice, assigned to suppress or destroy priority or hard-to-kill targets with high-angle fire. Our M.G.s were used to focus on smaller but critical targets or areas about the size of a small house and blast it with a cone of either direct or indirect fire.

We were finally making some headway against *KRIEMHILDE*.

Revived by a few hours of uninterrupted sleep and a hot meal, Oct. 8 found us in the 159th Inf. Brig. in better spirits and we steeled ourselves for any eventuality. "Army Hard" or "As tough as a British cracker," we called it. Others would simply repeat: "You're in the Army now, you're not behind a plow, you'll never get rich, you son-of-a-bitch, you're in the Army now."

While we were behind the lines conducting recovery operations near Cuisy and the 160th Inf. Brig. was preparing to breach *KRIEMHILDE* in the vicinity of Cunel, French and British armies, farther north, were making similar gains in Champagne, Picardy, and Flanders. "Just one more push" it was hoped, and we'll be pissing in the Rhine by Christmas! Joe Latrinsky was also telling us that Germany was in a state of rebellion due to starvation and heavy losses. Of course, this was only Joe talking, but we all liked Joe and, more importantly, felt it first hand at the front as we heard it from the German captives. When we overran their positions, we noticed that their tan canvas haversacks, which they usually wore on the back of their belts, were empty of provision. Hun troops at the front were in fact starving and if they were, it is "fer sure" that the homefront was, too, especially considering the general make-up of the German Imperial system.

During our *Interregnum* from the front lines, Cronkhite and Jamerson issued the following citations to the officers and E.M. of their respective commands:

---

[93] *Malaumont* is pronounced "Mal-ah-moan."

HEADQUARTERS EIGHTIETH DIVISION, A.E.F.

7 October, 1918.

To the Officers and Men of the 159th Brigade:

The Division Commander wishes to express his great appreciation of the highly important successes gained by Brig. Gen. Jamerson's 159th Brigade and Major Montague's attached battalion of the 319th Infantry.

Continually under effective artillery fire on your flank, as well as machine gun fire from your front and flanks, you nevertheless returned again and again to the attack until your objective was gained and held.

Your success has earned the repeated congratulations of your Corps Commander as well as the thanks of your Country.

ADELBERT CRONKHITE.

Major General, Commanding.

> HEADQUARTERS 159th INFANTRY BRIGADE, A.E.F.
>
> 8 October, 1918.
>
> The Brigade Commander desires to add to the above his expression of appreciation of the work accomplished by the Brigade and by major Montague's Battalion, 319th Infantry, during the three days' fight for the BOIS DE OGONS, and his pride in the command of an organization possessed of that iron will and determination which alone could win success in the face of such odds.
>
> G.H. JAMERSON.
>
> Brigadier-General, Commanding.

Later in the day, the 159th Inf. Brig. was moved three miles southwest into Bois Montfaucon, the same location that the 160th Inf. Brig. had refitted the week before, *via* the bombed-out town of Malancourt. Along this route, we passed through several artillery and M.G. units as well as ammunition and supply trains that were tirelessly bringing much-needed *matériel* to the front. This march was made without interruption and by early afternoon the men of the regiment had our "bivies" up among the shattered trees and fallen timber. Luckily for me, ole Albert Getz was still above ground and we again shared a shelter tent.

Once established, we were instructed to continue recovery operations, which also included the assimilation of scores of new infantry lieutenants, fresh from the O.T.C. at Langres, and to be ready to move at a moment's notice. Just before we settled in for the night, however, we were informed that the entire upper echelon of the 159th Inf. Brig. had been sacked—that "the house was cleaned out." We understood why Col. Howard Perry was relieved—right or wrong, good or bad—but did not quite understand why our very own Col. Ulysses Grant Worrilow, the popular commander of the 318th Infantry, was relieved. Our brigade commander, Brig. Gen. George H. Jamerson, who had commanded our brigade since April 1918, had broken his foot just south of Bois d'Ogons, and was sent to the rear to recover. Assuming that Jamerson's absence would be short, Cronkhite chose to directly command the 159th Inf. Brig., acting through the brigade adjutant, Lt. Col. Edmund A. Buchanan, who simply passed Cronkhite's orders along to the regimental commanders. Col. Worrilow was replaced by Lt. Col. Charles L. Mitchell and Col. Perry of the 317th Infantry was replaced by Lt. Col. Charles Keller. They were the ones who got us across the final line.

October 9, 1918.

Weather: Misty.

Roads: Muddy.

On Oct. 9, General Pershing ordered his corps commanders (Liggett, Bullard, and Cameron) to renew their attacks against *KRIEMHILDE*. Being in the center, we in the 3rd, 4th, and 80th Divisions were designated as the American First Army's main effort and as such, received Pershing's reinforcing artillery. As before, the 80th Division, this time, Brett's 160th Inf. Brig., was to attack "hey-diddle-diddle-right-up-the-middle" through Ferme Madeleine and the Valley of Death while the 3rd and 4th Divisions enveloped Cunel, the army's main objective, from the east and west.

Right or wrong, Pershing pretty much terrorized his corps commanders to keep pushing north toward Sedan no matter the cost, who, in turn, terrorized their division commanders to do the same. Although we never heard these strong words *per se* (e.g., "no matter the cost"), we certainly felt the pressure, esp. those in the infantry regiments. But then again, what was Pershing supposed to do? He understood the big picture and we didn't. He was the one getting the reports from signal scouts in the air about what was really in front of us. We in the Infantry really only moved at night and when we attacked during the day, we could only see things in a 500 x 500 yard box—if that.

On Oct. 9, Liggett's American I Corps, now including the famous 1st Division, backed by an infantry brigade from the 91st (Wild West) Division, was to attack Côtes Romagne from the west. To Liggett's right was Bullard's American III Corps, which had the 3rd Division on the left, the 80th Division in the center, and the 4th Division on the right, with the 5th (Red Diamond) Division in reserve. In the Rock of the Marne Division's sector, the 38th Infantry was to attack on the left and the 30th Infantry was to attack on the right. On the 3rd Division's right was the 80th Division's 319th Infantry (3/319 as the attack battalion, 1/319 as the support battalion, and 2/319 as the reserve battalion). To the 319th Infantry's right was the 320th Infantry with 1/320 as attack, 3/320 as support, and 2/320 as reserve ("attack in depth" and "defend in depth" were our mantras). We were to attack *en echelon* from the left: The 3rd Division was to attack first, then the 80th Division, and then the 4th Division.

Under this scheme, the 160th Inf. Brig.'s attack time (H-Hour) was contingent upon the progress of the 3rd Division, just as the 4th Division's attack time was dependent upon the 80th Division. Reportedly, the forward units of the 3rd Division were a km ahead of the 319th Infantry on the left, holding Bois Cunel, and the 4th Division was a kilometer ahead of us on the right, occupying Bois de Fays up to the Cunel-Nantillois Road. It will be remembered that the western part of Bois Fays originally had been in the 80th Division's sector and had been seized by we in Maj. Sweeney's 1/318 on Oct. 5.

From the map, then, Brett's 160th Inf. Brig. would be protected on both flanks for at least a km, between Bois Cunel and Fays. The open ground between the two woods was bad enough—we called it "the Valley of Death"—especially around *Ferme Madelaine*. At 3:00 P.M., H-Hour for the 160th Inf. Brig. was announced for 3:30 P.M. At 3:15 P.M. there was to be a fifteen-minute artillery barrage on an east-west line just north of Ferme Madeleine and then a rolling barrage was to cover the advance.

At 3:30 P.M. with the 320th Infantry on the right and the 319th Infantry on the left, hugging the Cunel-Nantillois Road, the 160th Inf. Brig. left the cover of Bois d'Ogons and attacked into the "Valley of Death." Capt. Gerald Egan's 3/319th Infantry was the designated attack battalion in the western sector with I/3/319 on the right and Company L/3/319 on the left, Companies M and K in support. It was followed by 1/319 and then 2/319.[94] Maj. Williams's 1/320th Infantry was the attack battalion in the eastern sector with B/1/320 on the right and A/1/320 on the left followed by Companies D and C, respectively, in support.[95] Behind them, stacked up by battalions, were Maj. Emory's 3/320, followed by Maj. Holt's 2/320. Lt. Lukens's platoon from I/3/320, being part of the support battalion, was assigned as one of the regiment's "combat liaison groups" or flank guards. Its primary mission was to connect with the right of the 319th Infantry and to take care of any enemy infiltrators who might squeeze through.

---

[94] *319th Infantry*, 33.

[95] *1/320th Infantry*, 112.

During this attack, Brett's 160th Inf. Brig. reached Ferme Madeleine in the "face of heavy fire."[96] Like us two days before, they fought through the familiar pattern of taking down well-supported M.G. positions and rifle trenches, climbing over, under, or through barbed wire or other entanglements, and endured multiple enemy artillery strikes, which vomited up earth and split men in two. Maj. Ashby Williams, the commander of the attack battalion (1/320) in the center of the corps axis of advance, remembered the intense Hun artillery and *Minenwerfer* barrages and the capture of scores of German prisoners:

It was a beautiful afternoon and it seemed a pity to spoil it with so much din of war and bloodshed... I passed by the post of Company D, over the ridge and through the wire, thence by Companies C and B. The latter company was just forming the battle line... In the meantime the standing barrage had come down and the shells from our artillery were going over our heads by the thousand... a music that was rudely marred by the discordant sound of the demoralizing whiz-bangs (the Austrian 88s), and the insistent trench mortar shells that the Boche was putting over... As I waited at the edge of the Bois des Ogons and saw my brave boys in battle line coming up the hill to meet whatever fate might have in store for them, calmly, stoically, and indeed, sadly, I looked on them in wonder and admiration, and my heart went out to them in pity and in sorrow. In such a time as this one knows, indeed, that "War is Hell." In a few minutes the remainder of the headquarters came up and... we moved from shell hole to shell hole to the southern slope of the ridge running east from the wood. Here I could perceive that my right flank companies had been held up just in front of me and I established headquarters which, for the time being, included myself and my adjutant, in a fresh shell hole and waited for further developments. I immediately sent out a messenger to Capt. Little, who was in command of Company B, in the right front, asking him for information of his situation, and in a short time received word that he was being held up by enemy machine gun fire in the edge of the Bois de Fays in our right front. I sent him word at once to take a patrol through the woods through the right and take the enemy guns from the flank, as I knew the general situation of the guns from the map and from the reports of the patrols of the day before... Immediately after sending this message I ordered the trench mortars and the one-pounders to come up to

---

[96] As cited in *319th Infantry*, 33.

take care of the Boche guns if they could not otherwise be reached. I remember Lt. Zouck as he came up with his trench mortars; he was full of eagerness to do what he was ordered to do, a smile playing always on his youthful face. It was good for him, poor fellow, that he did not know that he had only one more day to live. I sent him and the officer in charge of the one-pounders to the edge of the woods at the crest of the ridge to be ready to give such fire as might be found necessary. In the meantime, I waited for action on the right flank... After about thirty minutes hold-up, [the enemy] opened on the ridge on which my troops and I were located with his trench mortars, those little six-inch monsters that shoot around thrity shots a minute, and with the demoralizing whiz-bangs, traversing from right to left and from left to right along the slope of the hill crest. The [Minenwerfer] shells, coming in rapid succession, were digging holes on each side of me the size of the one that I was in, and the merciless whiz-bangs were going over the parabola of the hill. The noise was so intense—noise of bursting shells, of the hideous crying of particles of flying steel - that I had to speak at the top of my voice to make myself heard by Lt. Preston, who was in the shell hole with me... A Boche prisoner who was sent by Lt. Pownall on the supposition that I might get some information from him was trembling from head to foot and could hardly speak. I saw at a glance that I could not get any information that was worth having from a man in his condition. I pointed to the rear... We never sent fighting men back with prisoners as we could not spare fighting men for this duty, unless there was a great body of prisoners.[97]

Lt. Edward Lukens of Maj. Emory's 3/320, positioned in support behind Williams's 1/320 with his platoon, remembered:

We advanced at a steady walk, while the Boche planes circled over our heads, and the shells tore holes in the earth around us. Our advance over this shell-torn field was a witness to the value of our open formation, and to our experience in quick dropping. Time after time a big one would come tearing through the air, a dozen men nearest it would drop, a cloud of earth and smoke would appear and one would wonder whether any of them had escaped. In an instant one would get up, and then another, and often the whole crowd would jump into their

---

[97] As cited in *1/320ᵗʰ Infantry*, 121.

places again, but sometimes one or two would lie still, or would rise slowly and start painfully toward the rear... Had we been in close masses, or had the men failed to drop flat when one landed in a small group, the battalion would have been blown sky-high. On the edge of the woods we saw a fearful spectacle. Phosphorus shells were breaking in air, throwing down blazing streamers of yellowish gray smoke in fantastic shapes, like weird monsters of death.[98]

By 6:00 P.M., the attack of the 160th Inf. Brig. brought it to a line about five hundred yards north of *Ferme Madeleine* along a German Army-built narrow-gauge railroad supply line, where they consolidated their position before they resumed their final (and epic) attack against *KRIEMHILDE*. Although "pauses" or "rests" in battle are not only needed but are also inevitable, ensure not to make them too long as the men will lose the "fire in their bellies" that is required to charge across an open field with bayonets fixed! In the railroad cut, company combat carts and water buffalos surprisingly came forward to replenish ammo and water (ammo wasn't much of an issue, as the men hadn't fired much—yet). Sanitary teams dealt with the wounded. Squad leaders and platoon guides reminded the men how to set their sights for 1,000 yards (set the leave sights at "10"), artillery liason officers started plotting targets, and battalion and company commanders positioned the supporting weapons.

When all was set, just before dusk, the battalion commanders blew their attack whistles, followed by the company commanders, followed by the platoon leaders and off the combat groups of the 160th Inf. Brig. went—charging up the low and clear ridge that was *KRIEMHILDE*. According to Capt. Peck of the F/2/319th Infantry, this attack "marked the beginning of the 'wildest night' in the history of the regiment." In order to try to flank the well-fortified and positioned Hun M.G.s of *KRIEMHILDE*, each company of the brigade apparently went its own way, crisscrossing the others' zones, some even moving into Bois Cunel, which was in the 3rd Division's area of operations. In so doing, a highly-trained, very-experienced German *Stoss* battalion, attacking east from Bois Cunel, infiltrated among the units of the 319th Infantry and "all hell broke loose" just north of the farm. Although the support and reserve battalions of 319th Infantry held their positions, it was, according to all who were there, a near thing.[99] Lt. Edward Lukens of I/3/320th Infantry remembered: "The situation was mixed up, and no one knew just where any other outfit was. Several companies of the 319th Infantry had apparently advanced

---

[98] As cited in *3/320th Infantry*, 82.

[99] As cited in *319th Infantry*, 33.

some distance ahead of us by 'sliding through,' that is, going past M.G. nests in the dark without clearing them out."[100] Maj. Williams, in command of the 320th Infantry's Attack Battalion, on the division right, experienced similar confusion. He writes:

> *In going over the map and by the use of the compass I could easily see that, in the darkness and confusion of battle and what not, my companies had to some extent lost their sense of direction and we were not heading with sufficient accuracy in the right direction for progress in the sector that had been assigned to us, and I determined upon a complete readjustment of positions before attempting further progress. Moreover, I was convinced that, unprecedented as it was, the peculiar situation here gave a fine opportunity for combing the Bois de Fays and Bois de Malaumont in my sector at night and clearing up my front to the Cunel-Brieulles road. Some of my company commanders were doubtful whether such a mission could be accomplished at night, but I believed it could, fully appreciating the difficulties of keeping contact in the woods at night, especially where men must fight for the most part hand to hand with the enemy. I therefore ordered Companies B and D to reform in the same order in which the attack was begun and to fall back about 300 yards to where a little trench railroad ran out of the Bois de Fays and to comb the latter woods to the ravine between the Bois de Fays and the Bois de Malaumont and to report to me when that mission was accomplished. This movement began at 9:30 P.M. Company C and one platoon of A Company I directed to await further orders. In the meantime I waited for developments… During the process of combing the Bois de Fays some of my men had captured a German corporal and they sent him to me. He had been in the war four years and was glad to get out of it. I asked him how many men were in the Bois de Fays and in the Bois de Malaumont. From what I afterwards ascertained it appeared that the information he gave me was correct. I also asked him the strength of the enemy along the ridge north of the Cunel-Brieulles Road, which I knew to be a strongly held enemy position. He said they were a thousand strong and a relief had taken place the night before, bringing in fresh troops. This was interesting if not cheerful news, although I could not afford to place too much credence in any statement he might make. I sent him happily on his way back toward Nantillois and suppose he reached*

---

[100] As cited in *3/320th Infantry*, 84.

there safely. At length, the mission given to Companies B and D of combing the Bois de Fays to the ravine having been accomplished in due time and many prisoners and guns having been taken, the company commanders reported to me.[101]

Confusion or not, Capt. Egan ordered his 3/319th Infantry to continue the attack. Always Move Forward! "Confusion is built into the plan!" we'd often joke. "It's part of the deception plan! If we don't know what we're doing, then neither will the enemy! It's in the *I.D.R.*!" We'd also say things like "Chaos is our friend!" or "Poor bastards! We've got them exactly where we want them—totally confused!" After several well-placed R.G. shots, one of Capt. Egan's platoons was actually able to break through *KRIEMHILDE* and Egan quickly funneled what was left of his battalion through the breach point like milk through a straw, charged up the road, and entered Cunel, capturing some two hundred Germans, including two Hun battalion H.Q.s!

The 319th Infantry Regiment of the 80th Division was the first American unit to breach *KRIEMHILDE*.

Let me say that again: *The 319th Infantry Regiment of the 80th Division was the first American unit to breach* KRIEMHILDE.

To reiterate, the 319th Infantry of the 80th Division was the first American unit to not only breach *HAGEN*, but also *KRIEMHILDE*, which was the prize.

Capt. Egan instructed his men to stuff the Hun prisoners into the church of the tiny, bombed-out town (which no longer exists), and ordered them to comb the entire area for the enemy while he waited (hoped) for the rest of Col. Love's 319th Infantry Regiment to arrive to help hold the place.

And then it happened.

American artillery, fired mostly from our very own 155th Arty. Brig., roared down upon the officers and men of 3/319th Infantry.[102]

---

[101] As cited in *1/320th Infantry*, 128.

[102] *313th Artillery*, 52-53 and *314th Artillery*, 40.

Of course, those in Capt. Egan's battalion didn't know for sure whose artillery it was—they simply knew that they were taking several casualties and that they were all alone in Cunel. With that, Egan ordered a retreat back to the farm, bringing his casualties with him. For all intents and purposes, 3/319th Infantry was considered *hors de combat* for the rest of the fight, and as such, became the regiment's reserve battalion.

Nevertheless, KRIEMHILDE had been breached, if only for an hour. And we in Cronkhite's 80th Division had done it, just like we had done it with HAGEN. And both times, it was Brett's 160th Inf. Brig. that had pulled it off. Maj. Ashby Williams, commanding the assault battalion of the 320th Infantry during the day's fight, summed up the battle in this manner:

> *We were fighting our way through the Kriemhilde-Stellung line, which was the third German main line of defense, which was made up of strongly defended and heavily manned positions which were supplied by a trench railway coming from back of the German lines, and we all knew that the Boche would hold this line to the last ditch, if possible... It was upon this line of defense that the Boche endeavored to hold up the advance of the great American Army through the Argonne Forest. A strong line of defense as this was, is a series of mutually-supporting positions. We had plowed our way through several of these mutually-supporting positions and were now face-to-face in our immediate front on the ridge east of Cunel with three heavily-manned and strongly-defended mutually-supporting positions.*[103]

The "mutually-supporting positions" that Maj. Williams denoted primarily emanated from the right in Bois Melaumont and Bois Fays. They shot enfilade fire from east to west into the 320th Infantry, which was moving north from Ferme Madeleine. The 320th Infantry, tasked with eliminating these strong points, had a hell of a time clearing Bois Fays let alone storming Bois Melaumont. On top of this, the Hun had O.P.s atop Côtes Cunel and had every square meter honed in for artillery strikes. We understood that the 80th Division was supposed to simply launch demonstrating frontal attacks—holding the Germans by the nose—while the 3rd and 4th Divisions, on our flanks, were actually to breach the line and conduct a double-envelopment. The problem was, however, that the 3rd and 4th Divisions couldn't break through, either.

---

[103] As cited in *1/320th Infantry*, 122-23.

October 10, 1918.

Weather: Misty.

Roads: Muddy.

On Oct. 10, Bullard's corps renewed its attack against *KRIEMHILDE* in the vicinity of Cunel, supported by guns from Heiner's 155th Arty. Brig., 80th Division. Although Brett's 160th Inf. Brig. held Ferme Madeleine and parts of Bois Cunel and Fays, "the Hun with the Gun" still held Bois Malaumont and Côtes de Cunel, the corps objective. Because of the terrain and enemy activity, no light batteries could be brought forward to act as accompanying artillery, offering direct fire support against the strong German positions. They did move farther north, however, establishing firing positions just south of Bois d'Ogons. During our post-war reunions, the Blue Ridge Red Legs reminded me that firing batteries had to be very careful as to how close they got to a tree line, as it affects the angle of a gun, thus curtailing its range. Too close, for example, and the guns have to be angled higher, thus targets of only "x-range" can only be serviced. Remember, the primary job of the artillery is to suppress or destroy enemy targets in support the Infantry. As such, the guns had to be positioned in order to actually hit those targets. Cover and concealment, although important, were thus secondary.

Once the 160th Inf. Brig. was set, Brett ordered it to attack *KRIEMHILDE* once again, heading for Cunel, in conjunction with the 3rd and 4th Divisions. Many of the educated men in the brigade likened the previous attack to A.P. Hill's dusk attack against Cemetery Ridge at Gettysburg on July 2, 1863, when the Confederates held the center of the Federal position, if only for a short time. This next attack, it was thought, would be "Pickett's Charge," and most of us knew how that turned out. While Maj. Wilfred Blunt's 1/319th Infantry would attack on the left soon after 10:00 A.M., Maj. Williams's 1/320th Infantry would attack on the right, each with two companies abreast and with attached supporting weapons (i.e., M.G.s, I.G.s, and mortars, which were always in the thick of the fight). 2/320th Infantry was assigned to support the attack of 1/319th Infantry and as such, the 320th Infantry attacked without a reserve.

As usual, the Germans were ready to meet them, and the attacking units were thrown back with heavy loss, especially from Hun "whiz-bangs." Maj. Ashby Williams of 1/320th Infantry remembered:

[I had] Capt. Barringer place his mortars in an open space in a ravine in Bois Fays, which was the only available location (he said) for the weapons with a view to bringing fire on the triangular Bois Malaumont...Whether by accident or whether they had information, I do not know, but almost on the instant that our barrage was laid down the Boche opened a counter-barrage which was the most intense bombardment I ever heard or experienced. His H.E. shells poured down on us like a monster hail storm, putting the candles out in my P.C. and shaking the place to its very foundation. I shall never forget that memorable morning. As I stood at the foot of the steps I remember the storm of bursting shells was so terrific I waited a few minutes hoping that the storm would break, but there was no let-up. [After the devastating barrage], I stepped out of my P.C. and literally walked over the top of dead men and a hundred feet from the place at the edge of the woods where I turned to the right towards the ravine. Dead men were lying everywhere. I remember particularly a group of 3 that had been killed by the concussion of one shell... The Boche artillery had indeed wrought terrible execution upon the American boys.[104]

Lt. Edward Lukens of I/3/320th Infantry similarly remembered:

Oct. 10 was a day full of mixed-up situations, moving back and forth and sideways with little accomplished, and shelling everywhere. Many a time that morning I cursed my job, and wished I was a "buck private" so that I could attach myself to any outfit I happened to meet instead of having to continue wandering around trying to learn the situation and find my own outfit... At one point I found myself in with the 4th Division [!], and thought of going forward with them to fight as a private, but reminded myself that I could do as a single extra man would not compensate for what might happen if a gap were left between the 319th and 320th Infantry Regiments, so I kept on combing the northern slope of Bois d'Ogons until I finally ran into our battalion and found that most of my men had landed there already, though some never did find it

---

[104] As cited in *1/320th Infantry*, 128.

and were used during the rest of the drive as stretcher bearers or ammunition carriers by the reserve companies that handled those jobs.[105]

To speak to Lt. Lukens's revelations about the difficulty of being a company-grade infantry officer in the U.S. Army during a war, it's a tough job—probably the toughest job in the world. Tougher, I would argue, than that of a field or general grade officer simply because of the time-in-grade (not much) and great responsibility involved. It must also be remembered, however, that those who choose to take on this responsibility, chose it. The Army never, ever, forced them to take a commission. Most of us privates, however, especially those from the "National Army" divisions, were forced into the Army by government decree. If you aren't up to the job, lieutenant or captain or major or whatever, then you owe it to the Army and those in your charge to return to the ranks. Conversely, it's not that easy being a private soldier, either. His pay is low, especially compared to that of a company grade officer's, his living conditions are always the worst the Army has to provide, and his life expectancy is low (although not as low as infantry lieutenants). Go no farther than check out a casualty roster: "Private, Private, Corporal, Private, Sergeant, Private, Private, Lieutenant, Private, Private, etc." Granted, there are for more privates in the army than lieutenants (about one to forty), and I know that by percentage Infantry lieutenants suffer far more casualties, but remember, nobody forced said lieutenant to take a commission.

Once again stopped cold by the strong German defenses along the Heights of Cunel, Brett's 160th Inf. Brig. fell back to the farm, with the H.Q. elements operating from Bois d'Ogons.[106] Maj. Williams remembered:

A strong line of defense, as this was, is a series of mutually supporting positions. We had plowed our way through several of these mutually supporting positions and were now face to face in our immediate front on the ridge east of Cunel with three heavily-manned and strongly defended mutually supporting positions. Upon the map they are designated as follows:

(a) A small triangular piece of woods located about 300 meters north of Cunel-Brieulles road, which triangle was heavily manned with machine guns

---

[105] As cited in *3/320th Infantry*, 85-86.

[106] *319th Infantry*, 34.

and with small artillery and flanked by small ridges on either side; (b) A system of enemy trenches about 300 meters north of the Cunel-Brieulles road and about 300 meters east of (a), which position was strongly held by machine gunners and riflemen, and (c) A strongly-held system of trenches on the ridge and in the edge of the Bois de Foret, about 300 meters north of (b). Those three positions, in addition to being strongly defended in themselves, mutually supported each other, and in addition were mutually supported also by a heavy volume of machine gun fire from the piece of woods over the rise to the west of our sector (d), by machine guns in the town of Cunel, and by a heavy volume of machine gun fire from the southeast edge of the [Bois Faux]. The three latter positions which mutually supported the enemy positions in my front were located in the sector of the 319th Infantry on my left. In addition to this flank fire from my left, there was also enemy flank fire from the south edge of the Bois de Foret in the sector of the 4th Division on my right. On the morning of October 10, therefore, I was attempting an advance upon information that my left flank was protected, but in reality it was completely exposed to fire from (d), from Cunel and from [Bois Faux], and with knowledge that my right flank was exposed. The latter situation was taken care of by my own dispositions. When my advance began, therefore, my left flank companies had not gone 200 yards north of the Cunel-Brieulles road before, coming over the edge of the slope, they were exposed to a murderous machine gun fire from the (d) position and from Cunel and [Bois Faux], all of which positions were on my left flank in the 319th Infantry sector. Moreover, those flanking enemy positions were able to hold up my left flank companies until the barrage had passed over the triangular position (a) in my front, and permitted the machine guns in that position to open on my troops from the front. It is needless to say that in the face of this murderous cross-fire it was suicide to advance further in that flank, and it therefore became necessary for my left flanking companies to withdraw into the woods just south of the Cunel-Brieulles road. I cannot speak too highly of the calmness and courage of my officers and men in the face of this difficult situation. The lines were reformed and company commanders directed to await further orders.[107]

---

[107] As cited in *1/320th Infantry*, 122-23.

In mid-afternoon, Cronkhite received the following message from Bullard's III Corps H.Q., announcing Pershing's "great dissatisfaction with the progress of the attacking divisions." It reads, in part:

> At 2:40 P.M. today the Army commander expressed to the corps commander his great dissatisfaction with the progress of the attacking divisions, taking into consideration the fact that the enemy is not now holding his front with sufficient strength to counterattack and is, therefore, very evidently holding it merely with successive machine gun positions. He directs, through the corps commander, that division commanders require brigade and regimental commanders to get in personal touch with front line conditions and see to it that energetic measures are adopted at once to reduce these machine gun nests. The Army commander is convinced that the enemy holds principally with M.G. groups, with little support in the rear, and that these groups can be reduced by aggressive action on the part of officers. The Army Commander also directs that ground once gained shall not be yielded, but on the contrary troops on the flanks will be pushed forward in support and also troops from the rear when necessary. The Army commander demands that the Brieulles-Cunel position be penetrated and captured.
>
> BJORNSTAD

If we would have seen this message during the fight, we may have marched right on up to Pershing, who we understood knew what combat was like, and said, "Then you do it!" Cronkhite was really good at shielding us from this nonsense, as was his job. Is it appropriate for one general officer to speak to another in the third person about "disappointment?" Yes, I guess (I'm not a general, nor ever will be one). Is this an appropriate communication from one general to another? Sure. Why not. We don't know whence Pershing got his information, but if his units were taking high casualties, then the enemy was clearly in strength. I'd understand his frustration if we were reporting 1% casualties—but we weren't. According to Lt. Lukens from I/3/320: "One high-ranking officer who was in the line told me the Corps Staff was a bigger obstacle in his way than the Boche."[108]

That night, as the men from the 160th Inf. Brig. licked their wounds, Heiner's artillery continued to pound away at the enemy. Pvt. Allen S. Hartman of H.Q. Company/314th Artillery was cited for bravery during this time:

> *On the night of Oct. 10, 1918, in the vicinity of Nantillois and during the particularly heavy concentration of enemy shell fire, Pvt. Hartman though already wounded, went to the assistance of a severely wounded infantryman, assisted in placing him on a stretcher and carried him to the first aide station. While carrying the stretcher Pvt. Hartman was again struck by a shell fragment.*[109]

October 11, 1918.

Weather: Cloudy.

Roads: Good.

Soon after dawn on Oct. 11, 1918, the 80th Division launched its forth attack (!) against *KRIEMHILDE* in conjunction with enveloping attacks from the American 3rd and 4th Divisions. Although this attack also failed to take Cunel ("the Army mission") the Blue Ridge Boys were able to finally secure Bois Malaumont. As before, the 319th Infantry, on the division left, attacked Côtes Cunel pretty much head-on and got slaughtered. The 320th Infantry, attacking on the division right through Bois Fays, however, was able to finally secure Bois Malaumont and push as far north as Bois Faux in conjunction with units from the Ivy Division.[110] Maj. Williams, still in charge of the attack battalion of the the 320th Infantry, was so low on men that he had to consolidate his four companies into two. He writes:

---

[108] As cited in *3/320th Infantry*, 86.

[109] As cited in *314th Artillery*, 45.

[110] *Faux* is pronounced "Foe."

My companies had been much depleted by casualties, and in order to be ready for the new attack when H-Hour should be announced, I reformed my battalion, putting Companies A and C into one company and drawing Company L from the support battalion, which latter company was placed in support behind Company D, so that the dispositions for the attack were as follows: Front line, Company B on left; Company D on right. In support, Company A (with Company C) on left; Company L on right... I had rations and water taken to the men, and men and officers alike took such shelter as they could find from the high explosive shells that never ceased to fall in our area. Late in the afternoon our own artillery was putting shells on my troops, no doubt by a misjudgment of the range and by a lack of observation, and I had to phone back and ask to have the firing stopped. During the afternoon a detachment was sent out toward the left front, and by infiltration took a machine gun that was established in a foxhole along the open ridge called St. Christophe and which had been giving us much trouble.[111]

Lt. Lukens of I/3/320th Infantry, coming up behind 1/320, similarly remembered:

At last the order came for a fresh advance, and in the morning we formed in the field in front of the farm and started up the hill, but had to wait again for a few minutes in shell holes while our artillery repeated the now-familiar process of shelling the wrong place. This lack of liaison with the artillery was our greatest handicap throughout the Cunel drive, as further events of that morning showed. We resumed the advance, and soon came in sight of the church tower of Cunel, only a km or so away, but between it and us were patches of woodland filled with M.G.s and field pieces as thick as pumpkins in a corn field. We had crossed over a protecting ridge in the field and were approaching one of these little woods, when the M.G.s opened up on us. We dropped flat, and started at once to advance "by rushes," or "filtering," a few men at a time jumping and running a few yards, then diving behind any slight swale they could find, like a baseball

---

[111] As cited in *1/320th Infantry,*

player sliding for a base, and so getting under cover before a gun could be sighted on them.[112]

In combat, we from B/1/318th Infantry acted similarly to Lt. Lukens's platoon from I/3/320th Infantry. I'm sure it was like this across the division, if not the entire A.E.F. What I mean by this is that we moved as a platoon "combat group" and each weapon-specific squad maneuvered forward by short rushes. Generally we'd say things like "I'm up, I'm seen, I'm down" to control how long we stayed up under fire. Other men would say things like, "Yankee Doodle Dandy." All of this was spelled out in the *I.D.R.* that we learned even while at Camp Lee. Our experiences with the British in Artois and Picardy and later, here, in the Meuse-Argonne, solidified the practice. The key is to get up to "the last 100 yards" as soon as possible with as many men as possible. After that, it becomes a platoon-level fight—at fifty yards, a squad-level fight, and after that, a buddy team fight. Never, ever train to expect to get any help from higher, as you'll simply get frustrated and upset. When help does arrive from higher—and it might if you're deemed to be important—then see it as a combination of Christmas and Halloween. We Doughs of the 80th Division, in fact of the entire A.E.F., cannot emphasize enough the importance of platoon-level training, as the platoon will be your war. Learn to attack, defend, move, recover, and utilize supporting weapons at that level. The company commander is, in fact, merely an expert platoon leader. He'll show up every now and then to provide some extra firepower or advice to the platoon leader, but remember, he has three other platoons to command with a battalion commander breathing down his neck, and not always in a good way. The same holds true for the battalion commander; consider him as an expert platoon leader with some nifty supporting weapons at his disposal. In short, once we crossed the L.D., our platoon, for all intents and purposes, was "alone and unafraid." That was the message the Army and General Pershing were trying to get across to us Doughs all along. The field grade officers, as agents of the Army, would provide the plan, the training, the guidance, the weapons, the food, the equipment, etc., but it was up to us at the company and platoon levels to actually win the battle and as Frederick the Great famously said: "Battles win wars."

As the violent contest progressed, the 320th Infantry linked up with elements of the 4th Division in Bois Faux. It was from Bois Faux where the high command hoped to finally breach *KRIEMHILDE* as the clear fields of fire of Côtes Cunel were just too deadly. The 319th Infantry and other units could attest to that fact. Lt. Lukens of I/3/320th Infantry, still assigned as the support battalion of the regiment remembered:

---

[112] As cited in *3/320th Infantry*, 87-88.

We emerged from Bois Malaumont at the northern edge without difficulty, for the woods had been already cleared except for a few snipers by the companies on our right, and we dropped into the ditch of the Cunel-Brieulles Road which ran traverse in front of the woods. Maj. Emory came up and ordered Lt. Dunmire's 1st Platoon to recon the patch of woods to our left-front... [We soon thereafter followed and advanced into Bois Malaumont], small though it was, and [lost contact with the 319th Infantry]. This gap was my concern, and the major sent me back to find its extent, and to see that no harm resulted from it. A whole platoon could no longer be spared from I/3/320th Infantry, so I took with me only a small patrol, consisting of Sergeant Sugden, Corp. Shay, and two or three privates. As we were going back, keeping just inside the cover of the woods, we ran into a streak of the strongest gas we have ever experienced. I do not know what kind it was, for it had none of the typical odors, but was rather anesthetic in effect, choking you like ether, and had we not instantly put on our masks we would have been quickly knocked out.[113]

But like the 319th Infantry, on the left, the 320th Infantry, on the right, could advance no farther. Cronkhite reluctantly reported this fact to Bullard, our corps commander. Cronkhite stated that the Blue Ridge Division was spent and that it could no longer be expected to breach *KRIEMHILDE*, especially given the fact that the Germans had stacked Côtes Cunel with some of their best units. Bullard surprisingly concurred and ordered the fresh 5th (Red Diamond) Division to replace the 80th Division in order to renew the attack (so much for "the enemy is not now holding his front with sufficient strength to counterattack and is, therefore, very evidently holding it merely with successive machine gun positions"). But the men of the 160th Inf. Brig. weren't out of the woods yet (no pun intended) and they had several more hours to endure real combat. Lt. Edward Lukens of I/3/320th Infantry remembered:

Our job now was not only to protect the gap [between the 319th and 320th Infantry Regiments], but at the same time to locate all the nearby companies so that we would be certain just how great the gap was and could judge how best to place our men. The 5th Division was to relieve us about midnight, so we knew that if we could keep the Boche from filtering back, for five or six hours more, our job would be done and we could shift our burden to the fresh troops with no

---

[113] As cited in *3/320th Infantry*, 90.

apologies. We were near to the limit of our physical strength, and but for this knowledge of the coming relief, we would have felt almost hopeless... As it was now quite dark, we decided to go around the edge of the woods in the open field; instead of attempting to use the trails through, and as we reached the southwestern edge of [Bois Faux], near the scene of our morning's skirmish, we could distinguish the figures of men lying in almost shell hole. I wondered what platoon this could be that, unknown to us, had come to help us fill our gap, and I went up to one group of them and asked in a whisper who they were. None answered, and thinking they might have fallen asleep at their posts, I shook one of them by the shoulder. Only then did I realize that I was speaking to a dead man, and every one of those men, who lay in their holes so naturally, facing the enemy as though still intent on defending their ground, had already finished their fight, and had been relieved ahead of us... [I eventually found the rest of my battalion in the woods and] there were still several hours to wait until our relief should come, and we lay still, watching and waiting with what patience we could muster. As our good luck would have it, nothing happened...other than Boche artillery was in action, and here again our luck was with us. An "Austrian 88," apparently not more than half-a-mile away, kept firing point-blank into the woods all night. Enough shells landed in the middle of that woods, at intervals of about 2 minutes, to have killed every man who lay in the fields north and west of the woods, and not a man there was hit by them. For hours we spent listening to them, and fervently praying that they would go on battering the empty woods and not change range or deflection... At last relief came. About 2:00 o'clock in the morning the companies of the 5th Division began coming in single file around the corners of the woods, guided by our runners. In silence we got up out of our shell holes and they dropped into them, and we filed out, away from out never-to-be-forgotten ["Valley of Death" and back to Ferme Madeleine].[114]

To better protect the shot-up 160th Inf. Brig. during its relief-in-place, Cronkhite wisely ordered the 314th M.G. Battalion (Mot.) to move a company onto Hill 274. The 314th M.G. sent its Company A with its six Ford "Specials" that carried the men, ammunition, guns, and

---

[114] As cited in *3/320th Infantry*, 96.

equipment to the southern slope of the hill where it established indirect fire positions to target the roads that led into Cunel.[115] Lt. Furr of the 314th M.G. Battalion remembered:

> *It was decided to place the twelve M.G.s of Company A in echelon on Hill 274, south of the woods, within easy reach of the infantry commander [319th Infantry Regiment] when needed. There was no doubting the seriousness of the fire, as the wounded were being carried back toward Nantillois on stretchers in a constant stream. The M.G. squads were placed in "fox holes" for protection against the artillery fire. In these positions one of the guns of the 3/A/314th M.G. was destroyed by a direct hit, but the marvel of it was that Corporal L.B. Smith and two men lying in the same hole with the gun, were uninjured. A battery of German artillery seemed to have a particular spite against the one hundred meters of ground occupied by this platoon, as it had no more than taken up the position when shells began falling here, and continued throughout the whole day to hit in approximately the same area. After the gun was blown up the platoon was moved a few hundred yards to the east and remained there without further mishap. As usual, toward dusk, the artillery increased in activity and the hills south of Bois des Ogons were given a general shelling, firing continuing until early morning, but the men were well dug in and were more fortunate than the artillery several hundred meters in the rear of the company, which had several casualties during the night.*[116]

Meanwhile, back in Bois Montfaucon with the 159th Inf. Brig., we continued to try to recover from the physical and psychological trauma of the previous battle as well as assimilate replacements, including my new platoon leader, Lt. Harry Ashby (Lt. Myers was wounded in Bois d'Ogons—like most other platoon leaders). Individually we were in almost as bad shape as we were by companies and battalions. It is a mistake to think that because a man is not wounded he is not affected physically and mentally by what he has undergone during combat. Fortunately, young men of sound constitutions have wonderful recuperative powers, and after a week or so more of sound sleep and hot food, they are usually "good to go." However, the long-term effects are telling as the war negatively affected the health of many of us, in varying

---

[115] *319th Infantry*, 34; *314th M.G.*, 42-43. The American 5th (Red Diamond) Division consisted of the 6th, 11th, 60th, and 61st Infantry Regiments and the 19th, 20th, and 21st Artillery Regiments.

[116] As cited in *314th M.G.*, 43-44.

degrees. For example, some of us became alcoholics, being forever haunted by the war. Some had lung problems from being gassed. Others suffered from rheumatism, the piles, etc. It must be remembered that when an Infantry outfit comes out of the line, it comes out hollowed-eyed, half-starved, and half-crazed. Most of us also had severe diarrhea because of the stress and bad diet. In other words, we were "all in."

At 4:00 P.M., orders were received for Jamerson's 159th Inf. Brig. to march to Fôret Hesse, a distance of some eight km to the south, back across Rui Forges, keeping off the road as much as possible.[117] My regiment was under way at 5:00 P.M. and in camp at 10:30 P.M. after having made a very strenuous hike across country—this area being a devastated "No Man's Land" of a continuous series of shell holes, destroyed trenches, and hidden wire. Here we were told that the entire 80th Division, minus its artillery brigade, would be consolodated for future action. The forest had numerous old French dug-outs from the battle of Verdun days, and that's where many of us chose to "cocoon up."

October 12, 1918.

Weather: Misty.

Roads: Muddy.

During the fight for *KRIEMHILDE*, "that evil witch-bitch" as we came to call it, from Oct. 5-11, the 80th Division suffered horrendous casualties. The number stood at 139 officers and 3,412 E.M., or about 18% of our assigned strength. The vast majority of the casualties, of course, were inflicted upon the infantry regiments and their casualty figures numbered closer to 50%.[118] Lt. Edward Lukens of I/3/320th Infantry later noted:

> *The fighting around this region was apparently not handled as well from above as was the initial stage of the drive. No such great barrage was prepared our way as was laid down on Sept. 26. Frequent changes of orders and uncertainty to just what we were supposed to do, incorrect artillery firing, and almost total*

---

[117] *Fôret Hesse* or "The Forest of Hessia" is pronounced "Four-et Hess."

[118] *317th Infantry*, 68.

absence of aviation, were annoying features. Lack of good "liaison" perhaps includes the others. Instead of preparing a coordinated attack, as on Sept. 26, and on Nov. 1, the staff apparently allowed each outfit to work out its own salvation, depending on the original impetus which had in fact been totally expended long ago. Some mistakes were made by line officers, but the greatest bungles were made higher up. In spite of everything, we gained ground, and in the course of time other divisions carried on until the Hun's death grip was loosened, but we took our turn in Hell to do it.[119]

During the night of Oct. 11-12, 1918, Brett's 160th Inf. Brig. was transported south to Fôret Hesse to rest, refit, and reorganize alongside their brothers from Jamerson's 159th Inf. Brig. after it was relieved by the 10th Inf. Brig., 5th Division, in the Valley of Death. Maj. Ashby Williams of 1/320th Infantry remembered:

I had not slept, except for a minute or two now and then from sheer exhaustion, and I had not shaved for over a week and must have looked as bad as I felt. But I am frank to confess that there was a spring in my step and, in some fashion, a sense of joy in my heart, and I noticed this in the step and voice of my companions, as we passed the Bois d'Ogons and out of that shell-swept area with its ever-present, nauseating odor of shell-gas and the horrible specter of dead and dying men, joy perhaps that I had not suffered their fate.[120]

As was S.O.P., the artillery regiments of the division remained in place, providing fire support for the newly rotated infantry units coming into their zones. Remember, according to Army doctrine: "the artillery is never held in reserve." For reasons that weren't totally communicated to us, on Oct. 12, Brig. Gen. George Heiner, the commander of the 155th Arty. Brig., was replaced by Col. Robert S. Welsh, his able operations officer. "Joe Latrinsky" told us that Heiner could not handle the stress of battle and that he was leaning too heavily upon Welsh, late of the 314th Artillery. Welsh was therefore officially given command of the brigade.[121]

To show you how things usually go, soon after the 9th Inf. Brig., 5th (Red Diamond) Division took over the zone in the Valley of Death at around 1:00 A.M., Walker's 314th Artillery

---

[119] As cited in *3/320th Infantry*, 78.

[120] As cited in *1/320th Infantry*, 137.

[121] Stultz, 497.

Regiment received "a hysterical report" from the *dilettante* Red Diamonds (this was their first real "Up the Line" experience—too bad for them!) that it was being attacked by Hun tanks coming down from the Heights of Cunel! In response, Walker ordered Lt. Raymond Shean's platoon from F/314th Artillery to move forward and destroy the tanks with direct fire while the O.P. called in a grid for indirect fire from the big guns of Col. Goodfellow's 315th Artillery.

Shean drove his guns as far north as the horses could go. Undaunted, he ordered the guns unhitched from their limbers in Bois d'Ogons and they advanced north through the dark, cut up woods by hand or "by prolong" (i.e., using ropes tied to the hubs with one horse). The problem with this method is that it's slow and, more importantly, one can only carry a few rounds of H.E. with them, the limbers and caissons being left to the rear. By the time the guns actually arrived to *Ferme Madeleine* (they had to be wheeled over or around scores of downed trees), it was daybreak and the Blue Ridge Red Legs discovered that the so-called German tanks were actually painted canvas shapes on frames mounted on farm wagons, objects which we called "Red Monkeys."

Needless to say, Shean's 2/F/314th Artillery stayed in place in case any real tanks arrived and prepared for the next push against *KRIEMHILDE*. During subsequent night's action, three soldiers from Walker's 314th Artillery were cited for bravery, Sergeant Charles G. Kleeh of Battery E and Privates George Spotts of Battery F, and William F. Garland of H.Q. Battery:[122]

> *On the night of Oct. 12, 1918, Sergeant Kleeh, under severe enemy shell fire, directed the moving of ammunition to the gun emplacements west of Nantillois. Sergeant Kleeh remained at his work encouraging the men under him until wounded.*
>
> *On the night of Oct. 12, 1918, Pvt. Spotts, after carrying a message to the infantry front lines, voluntarily made 2 more trips over the Cunel-Nantillois Road, which was subjected to continuous enemy shellfire.*
>
> *On the night of Oct. 12, 1918, Pvt. Garland was ordered to carry an urgent message from the regimental P.C. near Monfaucon to the battalion P.C.'s one km north of Nantillois. Pvt. Garland was severely wounded in the shoulder near*

---

[122] As cited in *314th Artillery*, 45.

Montfaucon, but refused to go to the hospital and delivered both messages before seeking surgical treatment.

October 13, 1918.

Weather: Cloudy.

Roads: Muddy.

The morning of Oct. 13 found those of us in 2/B/1/318th Infantry in fairly good spirits (all things considered). We'd had at least two nights of relatively uninterrupted sleep, hot chow, the sounds of battle were distant, and life in *Fôret de Hesse* wasn't all that bad. It did take several days before most of us got rid of a chronic tired feeling, however. Within an hour after breakfast, for example, we would feel as though we had done a full day's work, and to walk a mile or two was still a burden. It also took several more nights before we could actually sleep soundly for a few hours straight without being awoken by the sound of incoming Artillery. At this point, an electrical fear had been ingrained into us that our bodies actually took years to recover, believe it or not (and some never did).

While in Fôret de Hesse, N.C.O.s continued to train the new E.M. and the squads, filled with replacements, slowly learned to act as a team. We were, in fact, almost an entirely new infantry company (if not battalion and brigade). Naturally, we did not start any very strenuous training right away, but gradually worked into it as our "pep" slowly came back. The irony is that the least experienced of us had the most energy while the most experienced had the least.

I guess it all evens out.

Our new platoon leader, Lt. Ashby, played it right. He mostly watched and listened. He learned who the key players of the platoon were and got to know our platoon guide, Sergeant Brown. I have to thank Capt. Douglas in large part for this, as he took an active interest, unlike other company commanders, in developing our platoon leaders. He did not simply push them off on the platoon guides. He understood that while the officers commanded the unit, the N.C.O.s commanded and looked after the men. As the *M.M.T.* said: "The officer is the owner and the N.C.O. is the foreman." For us that meant that the company commander was the owner, the platoon leader was the owner's son, the platoon guide was the foreman, and the squad leaders were his muscle.

We also understood that company-level officers didn't have to know everything (but a lot) and they didn't have to be the strongest, the fittest, the fastest, or even the smartest. But they had to represent the Army and at least attempt to model its high standards. They were the Army to us, like it or not. We expected our officers to know Army Regulations backwards and forwards. For us, that meant that they not only had to know what was written in the *I.D.R.* and the *F.S.R.*, but also how to properly *teach and apply* their principles. They had to lead, setting the example as articulated in the *I.D.R.*, all of the time. Whether they liked it or not, officers were "the book" to us and they were always being watched and evaluated by the N.C.O.s and E.M. They had to know how to take the soldiers that the Army entrusted to them and form them into an unbreakable team. Not the fastest? Fine, then be fast enough find who is and train that soldier to do those jobs that require speed. Not the smartest? Then be smart enough to find out who is and train that soldier to accomplish those tasks. I don't mean to trust everyone, either. There will always be somebody, especially in the N.C.O. corps, who will try to bring an officer down, even at the expense of the unit or the mission.

Company-grade officers, especially those in the infantry, cavalry, or artillery branches, have to be brave. Again, it doesn't mean that they have to earn a D.S.C. during every mission, every day, or at all, but they have to be there—they have to learn to control their fears and be in charge of the unit/situation or else somebody else will be. And once somebody else takes over, that officer is no longer in charge, and it will be very hard to regain the respect of his subordinates again, especially if engaged in combat, which is the *sine qua non* of the Army. Granted, I was just a lowly A.R.-man during the war, but I watched and I learned from the best. After the war, in 1926, I chose to became an Army Reserve infantry lieutenant and am currently (1938) an assistant regimental operations officer with the 317th Infantry, which is based in Richmond (more on that later), with the rank of major. According to the Army, the following is mentioned about "Leadership":

> *I.D.R. 358. The art of leadership consists of applying sound tactical principles to concrete cases on the battle field. Self-reliance, initiative, aggressiveness, and a conception of teamwork are the fundamental characteristics of successful leadership.*

I.D.R. 359. A correct grasp of the situation and a definite plan of action form the soundest basis for a successful combat. A good plan once adopted and put into execution should not be abandoned unless it becomes clear that it can not succeed. After thoughts are dangerous, except as they aid in the execution of details in the original plan.

I.D.R. 360. Combats that do not promise success or some real advantage to the general issue should be avoided—they cause unnecessary losses, impair the morale of one's own troops, and raise that of the enemy.

I.D.R. 361. Complicated maneuvers are not likely to succeed in war. All plans and the methods adopted for carrying them into effect must be simple and direct.

I.D.R. 362. Order and cohesion must be maintained within the units if success is to be expected.

I.D.R. 363. Officers must show themselves to be true leaders. They must act in accordance with the spirit of their orders and must require of their troops the strictest discipline on the field of battle.

I.D.R. 364. The best results are obtained when leaders know the capacity and traits of those whom they command—hence in making detachments units should not be broken up, and a deployment that would cause an intermingling of the larger units in the firing line should be avoided.

I.D.R. 365. Leading is difficult when troops are deployed. A high degree of training and discipline and the use of close order formations to the fullest extent possible are therefore required.

I.D.R. 366. In order to lighten the severe physical strain inseparable from infantry service in campaign, constant efforts must be made to spare the troops unnecessary hardship and fatigue—but when necessity arises, the limit of endurance must be exacted.

I.D.R. 367. When officers or men belonging to fighting troops leave their proper places to carry back, or to care for, wounded during the progress of the action, they are guilty of skulking. This offense must be repressed with the utmost vigor.

I.D.R. 369. The post of the commander must be such as will enable him to observe the progress of events and to communicate his orders. Subordinate commanders, in addition, must be in position to transmit the orders of superiors. Before entering an action the commander should be as far to the front as possible in order that he personally may see the situation, order the deployment, and begin the action strictly in accordance with his own wishes. During the action, he must, as a rule, leave to the local leaders the detailed conduct of the firing line, posting himself either with his own reserve or in such a position that he is in constant, direct, and easy communication with it. A commander takes full and direct charge of his firing line only when the line has absorbed his whole command. When their troops are victorious, all commanders should press forward in order to clinch the advantage gained and to use their reserves to the best advantage.

I.D.R. 370. The latitude allowed to officers is in direct proportion to the size of their commands. Each should see to the general execution of his task, leaving to the proper subordinates the supervision of details, and interfering only when mistakes are made that threaten to seriously prejudice the general plan.

A.D.R. 1499. The greater part of any field artillery command goes into action and remains under the immediate control of responsible officers. However, in reconnaissance work, in the ammunition supply service, and even in the batteries when communications fail; or emergencies suddenly occur, subordinates will be thrown upon their own responsibilities. Subordinates must therefore be given great latitude in the execution of their tasks. The success of the whole depends largely upon how well each subordinate coordinates his work with the general plan.

A.D.R. 1500. In a given situation it is far better to do any intelligent thing consistent with forceful the execution of the general plan than to search hesitantingly for the ideal. This is the true rule of conduct for subordinates who are required to act upon their own initiative. A subordinate who is reasonably sure that his intended action is such as would be ordered by the commander, were the latter present and in possession of the facts, has enough encouragement to go ahead confidently. He must possess the loyalty to carry out the plans of his superior and the keenness to recognize and seize opportunities to further the general plan.

A.D.R. 1501. Initiative must not become license. Regardless of the number of subordinates who are apparently supreme in their own restricted spheres, there is but one battle and but one supreme will to which all must conform. Every subordinate must therefore work for the general result. He does all in his power to insure cooperation between the subdivisions under his command. He transmits important information to adjoining units or to superiors, and, with the assistance of information received, keeps himself and his subordinates duly posted as to the situation.

A.D.R. 1502. When circumstances render it impracticable to consult the authority issuing an order, officers should not hesitate to vary from such order when it is clearly based upon an incorrect view of the situation, is impossible of execution, or has been rendered impracticable on account of changes which have occurred since its promulgation. In the application of this rule the responsibility for mistakes rests upon the subordinate, but unwillingness to assume responsibility on proper occasions is indicative of weakness. Superiors should be careful not to censure an apparent disobedience where the act was done in the proper spirit and to advance the general plan.

As we concluded our recovery operations in Fôret de Hesse, the artillery of America's Blue Ridge Division continued its support of the Red Diamond Division, which was slugging it out against *KRIEMHILDE* at Cunel, and repelling a strong German counter-attack in the Valley of Death (welcome to the war, "Fightin' Fifth!"). 1/313th Artillery reported: "Positions heavily shelled in early morning. Repulsed counter-attack at 16.00h. Reported our barrage very effective in breaking up the counter-attack and catching the Germans when attempting to return to their own lines."[123] During the day's fight, the 314th Artillery suffered five casualties, including Lt.

---

[123] As cited in *313th Artillery*, 158.

Robert Ober of B/314, who was K.I.A.[124] For their actions during the savage enemy barrages, Lt. Ober and Pvt. Royal W. Wynings of A/1/314 were cited for conspicuous gallantry:[125]

On the afternoon of Oct. 13, 1918, Lt. Robert Ober was directing the barrage of B/314 Artillery, at the battery positions north of Nantillois. In the course of the barrage the battery was spotted by a German aeroplane and the fire opened by the German battery with which the aeroplane was working. The first enemy shell which fell made the accuracy of the German adjustment obvious to all at the battery position. In spite of this fact, Lt. Ober continued to direct and encourage his gun crews. The example of his bravery and coolness inspired his men to forgetfulness of their own danger and a better performance of their duties.

Pvt. Wynings, telephone lineman, maintained telephone communication the entire night of Oct. 13, 1918, between his battery position and the battalion P.C. near Nantillois. Although the field between the two P.C.s was under terrific enemy shell fire and the telephone lines were almost completely destroyed several times. Pvt. Wynings did not allow communications to be interrupted for more than a few minutes.

October 14, 1918.

Weather: Rain.

Roads: Poor

Oct. 14 meant two things to the 80th Division: the great news that the American First Army had finally broken *KRIEMHILDE* at Cunel *via* Bois Melaumont and *Village Romagne* and the Blue Ridge Division's movement south to *Pretz-en-Argonne*, where we received new equipment, namely, brand-new Browning M1918 Automatic Rifles (B.A.R.).[126] According to the "War Diary"

---

[124] *314th Artillery*, 40.

[125] As cited in *314th Artillery*, 44.

[126] *Pretz-en-Argonne* is pronounced "Prey awn Are-gone."

of the 314th Artillery: "After an elaborate artillery preparation, the infantry attack [of the 5th Division] was launched at 8:30 A.M. We assisted the 313th Artillery in delivering accompanying fire which rolled north across Cunel."[127] During the attack, the 313th Artillery suffered ten casualties when a gun from A/1/313th Artillery was hit by a Hun H.E. round. During the momentous attack, the 32nd (Red Arrow) Division breached *KRIEMHILDE* at Romagne on the left and the 4th and 5th Divisions breached *KRIEMHILDE* on the right, plowing into Cunel from the east (the breach at Romagne earned the 32nd Division the moniker, "Breakthrough"). With that, the American First Army did the impossible: it breached *KRIEMHILDE*, one of the strongest defensive systems the world had ever seen! After this, there was only one formal German line left, *FREYA*, which was up near Barricourt and Buzancy.[128] And after that, it would be "Open Warfare" that Pershing often talked about (and emphasized), and we'd then be performing what is called "Pursuit Operations."

The momentous day started for us in the 318th Infantry at 5:30 A.M. when we were ordered to march south from Fôret Hesse through Esnes to Montzéville. There we were trucked south through Béthelainville and Sivry-La-Perche to Pretz-en-Argonne where we were to continue recovery operations (we loved recovery operations) in the adjoining villages of Vaubecourt, Sommaisne, and Beuzee. While billeted in barns and houses of Pretz-en-Argonne, we received a new issue of clothing, including brand-spanking-new wool overcoats! It was like Christmas times five, as it was the first time in many months that I felt this clean! Every stitch of clothing, from my socks and underwear to my tunic, trousers, putties, and field cap were brand new!

We A.R.-men also received new "Browning Automatic Rifles" (B.A.R.s). Unlike the "Sho-sho," which is made of stamped metal, the B.A.R. is solid. It weighs around sixteen pounds, has a twenty-round box magazine that fires, just like our M1917 Enfields and American Chauchats, 30.06 caliber rounds (but this time, well). It has an effective range as far as one could see out to 2,000 yards (in battle, we could only really see out to two or three hundred yards). We were taught to fire three-to-five-round bursts while walking forward ("moving fire") and when the magazine ran out of rounds, to take a knee, reload with the help of an assistant, and then continue the attack. The assistant would hand the gunner a new magazine while the gunner gave

---

[127] *314th Artillery*, 40.

[128] *Freya*, Wotan's wife, is pronounced "Fray-yah," *Barricourt* is pronounced "Bar-ree-core," and *Buzancy* is pronounced "Booze-awn-see."

him the empty one. We loved the B.A.R. so much that we thought that *every other* Dough should be armed with one!

The American First Army's strength was so reduced by mid-October that General Pershing ordered that the rifle companies be reorganized on the basis of four platoons, eight half-platoons or "combat groups," and 27 squads. Recent experience had demonstrated that the platoon-sized combat groups used in the previous drives (i.e., four task-specific squads) did not possess enough flexibility for the attack. The new formation called for a platoon of sixty soldiers, one commissioned officer and fifty-nine N.C.O.s or E.M., that was divided into two combat groups or "half-platoons" of three squads each (one A.R./R.G squad, one bomber squad, and one assault squad). While each squad was to be commanded by a corporal, each combat group was to be commanded by a sergeant. This was new because before, the platoon was our "combat group" and it had four squads performing separate but complementary tasks, all under the *aegis* of the platoon leader. Now we would have two co-equal combat groups per platoon, each led by a sergeant, which had three squads of mixed weapons and capabilities. With the new organization, each A.E.F. infantry company had around 250 Doughs, each infantry battalion around 1,000, each Infantry regiment around 3,000, and each infantry brigade around 6,000. This, of course, did not include attachments from the sanitary, quartermaster, ordnance, artillery, or signal corps.

My platoon, 2/B/1/318th Infantry, was commanded by Lt. Harry Ashby, a newly-minted "90-Day Wonder from Langres" who was once an N.C.O. from the 317th Infantry. Our platoon guide was still Sergeant Brown, who would help Lt. Ashby lead the platoon and steady the men. My combat group was commanded by newly-promoted Sergeant "Fightin' Bill" Murray, and it had three squads. My squad, the 3rd Squad, one of the A.R. and R.G. Squads of the platoon, was led by Corporal John Zubal, a man who I would follow into hell itself (and had!), and who was armed with an M1917 Enfield Rifle. The squad itself had two teams. Team One consisted of Private First Class (P.F.C.) Joe Riddle (me), who was the designated B.A.R.-gunner, P.F.C. Albert Getz, who was my assistant gunner (A.G.) and general "partner in crime," and P.F.C. James Stewart, who was the B.A.R. ammo carrier (bandoliers and a canvas satchel filled with B.A.R. magazines). Pvts. Earl Andrews and Wort Wise were our important R.G.ers and Jim Bruce and Boss Atkins were their ammo carriers/designated marksmen. Team Two consisted of P.F.C. Ben Schuyler who was the B.A.R.-man, P.F.C. Richard Grubbs, who was the A.G., Thornton Ridinger who was the B.A.R. ammo carrier, John Spratt and William Dunlap who were the R.G.s, and Harry Harmon and Larry Parker who were the R.G. ammo carriers.

Each B.A.R. gunner and his A.G. carried at least two B.A.R. magazine bandoliers that were crisscrossed over their shoulders, looking much like Pancho Villa. Each bandolier carried ten magazines and each magazine weighed about three pounds. The B.A.R. ammo carrier also sported bandoliers as well as a canvas satchel that was filled with another ten or so box magazines. That means that each B.A.R. team carried at least 1,500 rounds of 30.06 ammunition to suppress or destroy enemy targets while on the move, which means that each A.R. squad/battle group had at least 3,000 rounds while on the move! And that ammo really weighed down the ammo carriers.

Our 1st Squad, one of the bomber squads of the platoon, was commanded by Corporal Thomas Merritt. It consisted of two teams of seven or eight men each, armed with M1917 Rifles and hand grenades. As before, they were to get within twenty yards of a designated target, usually a concrete and camouflaged Hun pillbox, throw their hand grenades from the prone or kneeling positions. Once they hurled their grenades, the 2nd Squad, one of the assault squads of our platoon, was to charge through the bombers and take the objective with rifle and bayonet. This squad was the type of squad that suffered the most casualties in the A.E.F. The men carried most of their rifle ammunition in M1903 Bandoleers and their grenades in satchels or sand bags. They were to re-load their rifles from their bandoleers first.

Ammunition Supply.

I.D.R. 550. Company commanders are responsible that the belts of the men in their companies are kept filled at all times, except when the ammunition is being expended in action. In the firing line the ammunition of the dead and wounded should be secured whenever practicable.

I.D.R. 551. Ammunition in the bandoleers will ordinarily be expended first. Thirty rounds in the right pocket section of the belt will be held as a reserve, to be expended only when ordered by an officer.

I.D.R. 552. When necessary to resupply the firing line, ammunition will be sent forward with reenforcements, generally from the regimental reserve. Men will never be sent back from the firing line for ammunition. Men sent forward with ammunition remain with the firing line.

I.D.R. 553. As soon as possible after an engagement the belts of the men and the combat wagons are resupplied to their normal capacities. Ammunition which can not be reloaded on combat wagons will be piled up in a convenient place and left under guard.

To help fill our T.O., the infantry regiments of the 80th Division received replacements from the 76th (Liberty Bell) Division, men from New England. It was "bad enough" that we had Pennsylvania "Yankees" with us, but now we had New England, Clam Chowder-slurping actual Yankees among us! Needless to say, we treated them coldly. Not necessarily because they were from New England (which didn't help) but because they were "fresh fish" who knew nothing of war (and this was coming from a crew that only served a couple of weeks in battle). Even worse, they were replacing our friends from Camp Lee who had been blown into pieces and these new replacements made us feel like our friends were nobodies—that they were easily replaced—that we were all expendable—just like a canvass pistol belt, a canteen, or other issue item.

But once the Liberty-Bell-turned-Blue-Ridgers survived their first engagement, they were "in like Flynn" and true-blue Blue Ridgers. The 314th M.G. Battalion (Mot.), arguably one of the more-important units of the division, received twenty replacements from the 40th (Sunshine) Division, men drawn mostly from California.[129]

During our time in the Meuse-Argonne, Pershing's American First Army apparently issued several "Combat Instructions" to the chain of command. At our level, of course, we never heard about them directly but were indirectly affected by them as the instructions were included in our operations. When I read them after the war, during the 1930s, I actually found them a little insulting. I was inspired when I read Pershing's *Experiences in the World War* (1931), but when I read some of the nonsense that came out of the "Instructions," my esteem for him dropped a little—not much—but a little. He'd often blame our "lack of forward movement" on fear or "lack of vigor."

Look, I was never a general. In fact, during the war, I was simply a lowly A.R.-man so I don't know what motivates general officers. But what I do know is that E.M. seek resources to do the job that includes leadership, guidance, and instruction. That's it. Officers: don't be a Degoutte or a Bullard—be a Cronkhite. Some of Pershing's instructions, for example, once again

---

[129] *314th M.G.*, 44.

pressed "the primacy of the rifle" and argued that our supporting weapons—A.R.s, R.G.s, M.G.s, I.G.s, mortars, etc.—were "merely adjuncts."

At our level, at least in Maj. Sweeny's 1/318 Infantry, we never heard this tripe. We in fact learned early on, starting with our time with the British in Artois, of the importance of "supporting" or "auxillary" arms. Does this mean that Infantrymen should not be trained to be as proficient as they can be with the rifle and bayonet? Certainly not—on the contrary. But Infantrymen also need to be trained how to operate and integrate supporting arms at all times. If not, they'll go pell-mell into hell with only a rifle, bayonet, hand grenade, and fork to simply be mowed down by deadly modern-day weapons.

Above all, infantrymen need to be taught to "Always Move Forward" with every means available as the modern battlefield is festooned with poison gas, shell holes, barbed wire—sometimes one hundred yards deep—H.E., shrapnel, bullets, and even aeroplanes dropping much of the same. To stay in place, especially in the open, will mean sure death. You can bet your life on that.

October 15-30, 1918

On Oct. 15, the Ottoman Empire, a member of the Central Powers, asked for an armistice (cease fire) because most of its possessions in the Levant and Mesopotamia had been over-run by British or French forces and it was engulfed in an internal insurrection that was led by Mustafa Kemal (Ataturk), a member of the Ottoman General Staff. For us in the infantry units of the Blue Ridge Division, however, this meant little as we continued to prepare ourselves in Pretz-en-Argonne for the up-and-coming attack north against *FREYA* (the Third Push). But again, it was a good sign. Keep on pushing and it will soon be over!

Welsh's 155th Arty. Brig. continued to support the Red Diamond Division that was operating in the area of north of Cunel until Oct. 22, when it was replaced by the 90th (Tough Hombres) Division. Welsh's brigade thereafter conducted hundreds of fire missions for the Tough Hombres, which, like the Red Diamonds, did not have an assigned artillery brigade. This attachment lasted until until Nov. 1, when the 155th Arty. Brig. was returned to the 80th Division south of Buzancy. On Oct. 15, 1918, P.F.C. Oscar Riggs of H.Q./314th Artillery was cited for conspicuous gallentry for helping to maintain communications among his battalion:

On the night of Oct. 15, 1918, being on duty at 1/314 O.P. near Cunel, P.F.C. Riggs volunteered to go out under intense enemy shell fire and heavy gas concentration to repair breaks in the telephone lines. In spite of the greatest difficulty he maintained communication throughout the night between the O.P. and the regimental central at Madeleine Farm. [130]

On Oct. 17, just a few days after Ottoman Turks dropped out, Pershing informed his new Army Group (American First and Second Armies, commanded by Lt. Gens. Hunter Liggett and Robert Bullard, respectively) that the Central Powers, conscious that they were losing (the Germans having shot their bolt with *Friedensturm*), were now begging for a cease fire. This meant that we had to continue to press the offensive vigorously in order that, under the plea for an armistice, the enemy may not gain time to restore order among their forces in order to recuperate. Pershing said: "There can be no conclusion to this war until Germany is brought to her knees."[131]

As far back as Aug. 8, when Hindenburg informed the Hun Emperor that "the war is lost," the Germans have been asking for an end to the war based on Wilson's Fourteen Points. The problem was that the Allies, meaning France, Britain, and Italy, wanted Germany, and especially its nobility, to pay. In exchange for peace, the Kaiser and Germany's entire noble coterie was to abdicate, Germany was to become a republic, the German Army was to abandon its artillery and retreat to the east bank of the Rhine, its fleet was to be turned over to the British, Alsace and Lorraine were to be returned to France, and the independent "Republic of Poland" was to be carved out of Old Prussia and the newly-conquered territories. This, the Germans were not quite willing to do (yet), and the war would go on (this is why it lasted until Nov. 11, 1918). According to *Reichsfeldmarshal* Wilhelm Groener, who replaced Hindenburg as the General-in-Chief of the German Imperial Army (*Erster Generalquartiermeister*) on Oct. 29, 1918:

The withdrawal of the front to the line "Antwerp-west of Brussels-Charleroi-Meuse River" had become necessary... But the decision had to be taken in clear recognition of the inevitable consequences, because our first duty is and remains that of avoiding under all circumstances a decisive defeat of the army. When

---

[130] *314th Artillery*, 45.

[131] As cited in Harbord, 449.

once the enemy breaks through, the danger of such a defeat is there, since the Supreme Command no longer disposes of reserves of the necessary fighting quality.[132]

Maximilian, the Crown Prince of Baden (Max von Baden), who became the German Imperial Chancellor (*Deutsches Reichskanzler*) or Prime Minister on Oct. 1, 1918 remembered:

As the result of this falling back of the northern sections of the army to the given line, [the army] would only hold out the prospect of avoiding serious engagement for perhaps a fortnight, and thus giving the exhausted troops a little rest. But since the new line was not finished building, the military situation as a whole would not be improved... But one thing more must not be allowed to happen: the American Army, or any considerable portion of it—must be prevented from advancing north of Verdun; the moment the fresh troops, who were far superior to our completely exhausted troops, advanced, it would be impossible to hold the position for long.[133]

On Oct. 22, the M1915 Colt-Vickers M.G.s of America's Blue Ridge Division were turned-in and replaced by brand-spanking-new M1917 Browning M.G.s, which were improved models of the Colt-Vickers. According to one M.G. officer, they "immediately became a favorite with the men."[134] Like the Colt-Vickers, the M1917 Browning M.G. is a crew served, belt-fed, water-cooled M.G. that fired 30.06 bullets at around 500 R.P.M. (or two belts of ammunition per minute). The M1917 M.G. had a range of about 4,000 yards in the indirect fire mode. Remarkably, Lt. Val Browning, the inventor's son, was sent by the Army to help train our M.G. platoons and to monitor the newly-fielded weapon "in action." Why we in the 80th Division were honored with the combat field-testing, I know not. We assumed that it was because Pershing had confidence in us and that we would put the new weapon to good use, as not all divisions received the water-

---

[132] *Ibid.*, 462. The ranks of general officers in the German Army, 1914-18, were: *Generalmajor* (brig. gen.), *Generalleutnant* (maj. gen.), *General der Infantrie*, or *Artillerie, Cavalrie*, etc., (or "of the branch"—lt. gen.), *Generaloberst* (Brig. Gen.), *Generalfeldmarschall* (the U.S. Army does not have equitable rank but it would be equal to an "Army Group Commander" like Pershing was during the last month of the war. Of the field grades, *Major* (maj.), *Oberstleutnant* (lt. col.), and *Oberst* (col.); of the company grades, Leutnant (2lt.), Oberleutnant (1lt.), and Hauptman (capt.).

[133] As cited in Harbord, 463.

[134] As cited in *314th M.G.*, 44.

cooled Browning M.G.[135] The reason why we had M1917 Enfiled Rifles and Colts-Vickers M.G.s, and not M1903 Springfield Rifles and Hotchkiss M.G.s, is because we came to France in the second wave. Those divisions in the first wave, the ones that were built around Regular Army or National Guard formations, were generally armed with Springfield Rifles and Hotchkiss M.G.s.

On Oct. 23, B/1/314th Artillery, providing fire support for the Tough Hombres, again received the command to move forward and take up a new position, under threat of a Hun infantry counter-attack. According to Capt. Beebe:

> *Our battery led the battalion and upon reaching Romagne it was reported from the front that the Germans had broken through the Infantry lines about four hundred meters off the road. So the battery pulled to one side and prepared for action, awaiting the command to fire point-blank at the supposedly on-rushing hordes of Huns. M.G.ers were called forward and placed in position and the gun crews were ordered to load their side arms. Later reports brought us the good news that the first report was either a false one or that the enemy changed his mind and the fact is they were definitely checked by the infantry.*[136]

On Oct. 24, 1918, Jamerson's 159th Inf. Brig. was loaded aboard scores of French *camions* and departed Pretz-en-Argonne for Islettes Petites in the Argonne Forest where the 77th (Metropolitan) Division had fought its way north while we were busy fighting our way up through Bois Septsarges and Brieulles a few days before.[137] Hitching a ride with a French motor transport unit is an experience in and of itself. Let's just say that speed in loading was not one of their priorities. This particular *camion* unit was commanded by French officers and N.C.O.s but was operated by four to five-feet-tall Vietnamese from French Indo-China who wore strange hats and goat skin coats. This truly was a world war! The sight and sound of these French-speaking southern (Indo) Chinamen threw us for a loop. Each rifle company was lined up along the road and ordered to count-off by sixteen. With that, the chosen sixteen were directed by a French-speaking Indo-Chinaman to load up aboard his *camion*. Our chain-of-command had nothing to do or say with the loading. After a few hours aboard *les camions*, catching as much sleep as we could, we arrived at *Islettes les Petites* at around 11:00 A.M. and were ordered to

---

[135] *317th Infantry*, 71.

[136] *314th Artillery*, 52.

[137] *Islettes Petites* or "Small Islands of the Tiny" is pronounced "Ees-lets Pet-eat-ays."

establish company bivi sites. Once again, my good friend and A.G., Albert Getz, was my tent mate.

We knew that we were to get ready for the next push and for the next week or so, the air was electric with anticipation of the coming attack, which all expected to be even more successful than the previous ones. The Associated Powers had been hammering *les Boche* for a month now without cessation and the whole battle line from the Meuse to the North Sea was on fire. While pessimists still existed who foresaw the war lasting into 1920, many, like me, were willing to bet (and hoped!) that the Hun would capitulate before the year was out.

On Oct. 27, five soldiers from the 314th Artillery, Corporal Clarence R. Sandy of H.Q. Battery, P.F.C. John Babbit of H.Q. Battery, Private Albert L. Tomblin of Battery A, Private Williard H. Groff of Battery C, and Private Chester Sprouse of the regimental supply company, were cited for conspicuous gallantry while conducting operations in the vicinity of Cunel-Romagne:

> *On Oct. 27, 1918, Private Groff, at ROMAGNE, while under exceptionally heavy shell fire from the enemy, carried messages between his battery and the battalion P.C. until severely wounded.*
>
> *On Oct. 27, 1918, Wagoner Sprouse was driving a wagon with rations to be delivered at the battery positions near ROMAGNE. The cart was hit by a shell and Wagoner Sprouse was wounded. In spite of the fact that the road remained under constant shell fire he continued his way, delivered his rations, and returned.*
>
> *On the night of Oct. 27, 1918, at the P.C. of 1/314 north of ROMAGNE, where all communication had been destroyed by enemy shell fire concentrated on the battalion telephone central. Telephone Corporal Sandy was ordered to have communication established at once. Rather than send out his men under the intense fire, he went himself, restored communication, and with the assistance of one man maintained it until the bombardment ceased. There were sixteen circuits leading into the central, all of which was cut at least three times during the bombardment.*

On the night of Oct. 27, 1918, at 1/314 P.C. north of ROMAGNE, where all communication had been destroyed by enemy shell fire, P.F.C. Babbitt, of his own accord, left the dugout and repaired all of the lines. This was especially difficult in view of the fact that the area in which the breaks occurred was subjugated to a constant interdiction fire and many wires were broken again immediately after they had been repaired.

On the night of Oct. 27, 1918, Pvt. Tromblin was lead driver of a caisson team which was hauling ammunition to the battery positions at ROMAGNE. A shell exploded on the road in front of his team, wounding Pvt. Tomblin and one of the other drivers. In spite of this fact, Private Tomblin continued with his team until a place of safety was reached. [138]

American 75mm artillery wailing away at a Hun target. Note the spend shell casings of the fixed ammunition. Blam! Blam! Blam!

On Oct. 28, Corporal Thomas H. White of H.Q./314th Artillery was cited for gallantry in maintaining effective communications, allowing his unit to maintain effective fires:

On Oct. 28-29, 1918, Corporal White (then P.F.C.), a member of 2/314th telephone detail, was on duty as a lineman at the battalion O.P., which was

---

[138] As cited in *314th Artillery*, 44-45.

located a short distance west of BOIS-DE-RAPPES. Corporal White was the only lineman on duty on a line about three kilometers long and without aid maintained communications by extraordinary efforts on his part. Corporal White was repairing the line continually from 9:30 P.M. until 4:30 A.M. and was in the midst of heavy shell fire from the enemy during this whole period. [139]

On Oct. 29, 1918, Col. Harry C. Jones superseded Lt. Col. Charles Mitchell as commander of the 318th Infantry, Mitchell being returned to being regimental X.O. A number of other officers also reported to the regiment, almost filling our T.O. This, coupled with the fact that we had some real veterans in our ranks, our company, battalion, regiment, brigade, and division was as ready for action as it never had been before.

M.M.T. 926. Fear. The emotion of fear acts more powerfully upon the feelings of the individual soldier than any other emotion, and it is also probably the most infectious. Fear in a mild form is present in every human being. Nature wisely put it there, and society could not very well get along without it. For example, we stop and look up and down a crowded street before starting to cross, for fear of being run over—in going out in the cold we put on our overcoats, for fear of catching cold. In fact, we hardly do anything in life without taking a precaution of some kind. These are all examples of reasonable fear, which, within bounds is a perfectly legitimate attribute of a soldier in common with other human beings. For example, we teach the men to take advantage of cover when attacking, and we dig trenches when on the defense, in both cases for fear of being shot by the enemy. It is the unreasoning type of fear that plays havoc in war, and the most deadly and common form of it is a vague, indefinite, nameless dread of the enemy. If the average man was to analyze his feelings in war and was to ask himself if he were actually afraid of being killed, he would probably find that he was not. The ordinary soldier is prepared to take his chance, with a comfortable feeling inside him, that, although no doubt a number of people will be killed and wounded, he will escape. If, then, a man is not unreasonably afraid of being killed or wounded, is it not possible by proper training and instruction to overcome this vague fear of the enemy? Experience shows that it is. If a soldier is suffering from this vague fear of the enemy, it will at least be a consolation to

---

[139] As cited in *314th Artillery*, 45.

him to know that a great many other soldiers, including those belonging to the enemy, are suffering in a similar manner, and that they are simply experiencing one of the ordinary characteristics of the human mind. If the soldier in battle will only realize that the enemy is just as much afraid of him as he is of the enemy, reason is likely to assert itself and to a great extent overcome the unpleasant feelings inside him. General Grant, in his Memoirs, relates a story to the effect that in one of his early campaigns he was seized with an unreasonable fear of his enemy, and was very much worried as to what the enemy was doing, when, all at once, it dawned upon him that his enemy was probably worrying equally as much about what he, Grant, was doing, and was probably as afraid as he was, if not even more so, and the realization of this promptly dispelled all of his, Grant's, fear. Confidence in one's ability to fight well will also do much to neutralize fear, and if a soldier knows that he can shoot better, march better, and attack better, than his opponent, the confidence of success that he will, as a result, feel will do much to dispel physical fear. By sound and careful training and instruction make your men efficient and this efficiency will give them confidence in themselves, confidence in their rifles, confidence in their bayonets, confidence in their comrades and confidence in their officers... It is a well-known saying that a man in battle frequently regains his lost courage by repeatedly firing off his rifle, which simply means that his thoughts are diverted by physical movements. This is no doubt one of the reasons why the attack is so much more successful in war than the defense, because in the attack the men are generally moving forward and having their minds diverted by physical motion from this vague dread of the enemy.

As was already stated, Lt. Gen. Hunter Liggett, the commander of the American I Corps, replaced Pershing to become the American First Army commander, which was operating in the Meuse-Argonne. Lt. Gen. Robert Lee Bullard, the commander of the American III Corps, became the new American Second Army commander, which was still operating in Saint-Mihiel. Pershing, as commander-in-chief of the A.E.F., now acted as the American "Army Group Commander." By war's end, the American Third Army would also be formed. That night, we finally received our operations order to breach *FREYA* in the vicinity of Buzancy.

1-3
P. C. HAMILTON.
A. E. F.

29 October, 1918.
15 hours.

SECRET.

FIELD ORDER NO. 27.
MAPS: (BUZANCY - VOUZIERES 1/20,000).
(BUZANCY 1/50,000).
(VERDUN - MEZIERES 1/80,000).

I. (a) The First American Army, while continuing its operation east of the MEUSE, will attack on its front west of the MEUSE in the near future. The I Army Corps will attack on its present front, with 3 divisions in line. The attack will be an enveloping one from the right. The high ground south of VERPEL will be carried on D day, with the object of driving to BOULT-AUX-BOIS upon further orders.
(b) CORPS BOUNDARIES: East: - VAUQUOIS (inclusive) CHEPPY (exclusive), CHARPENTRY (inclusive), BAULNY (inclusive), EXERMONT (exclusive, FLEVILLE (inclusive), SOMMERANCE (exclusive), ST. GEORGES (exclusive), thence along 300th meridian to ridge just north of IMMECOURT, thence northeast along ridge between BAYONVILLE and SIVRY lez BUZANCY, FOSSE (exclusive), VAUX en DIEULET (inclusive). West: - No change.
(c) The 2d Division (V Army Corps) will attack on the right of, and the 77th Division will attack on the left of, the 80th Division.
(d) Troops attached to the 80th Division:
157th Field Artillery Brigade.
2 Batteries 65th C.A.C.
6 Batteries 247th R.A.C.P.(Fr.).(From H plus 2 hours, D Day to 0 hour, D plus 1 day).
219 R. A. C. P. (Fr.)
1st Aero Squadron
2d Balloon Company (also with 77th Division)
2 Companies 53rd Pioneer Infantry
Co. E, 1st Gas Regiment

II. GENERAL PLAN:

(a) Mission and Zone of action of the 80th Division:
The 80th Division will cover the left of V Corps. It will seize the high ground to the north of SIVRY LEZ BUZANCY on the first day.
Right (east) limit: - Same as limit of the Corps.
Left (west) limit: - APREMONT (inclusive), CHATEL CHEHERY (exclusive), CORNAY (exclusive), meridian 298 from the AIRE River to the western edge of BUZANCY, thence north to ST. PIERREMONT (exclusive).

(b) The objectives are those portions of the Corps Objective lying within the zone of action of the 80th Division, as follows:
1st Objective: IMMECOURT (exclusive)-ALLIEPONT (inclusive)
2d Objective: MALMY - SIVRY LEZ BUZANCY (inclusive-298.0-291.2
Corps Objective: FME. DES PARADES-COTE 278-299.0-293.0
Subsequent Objective: Ridge west of FOSSE-BUZANCY-HARRICOURT.

(c) Initial disposition for the attack will be with attacking Brigade with regiments side by side, each regiment in column of battalions.

(d) General direction of the attack: True north, (compass bearing 13 degrees east of north), to the 2d Objective.

(e) Upon reaching the Corps Objective patrols will be pushed well to the front preparatory to a further advance on the second day. The Corps Objective will be gained before dark D day.

III. DETAILED INSTRUCTIONS FOR UNITS:
(a) 1. The 160th Brigade will be the attacking Brigade.
Attached troops:
1 battalion Field Artillery.
1 company 305th Engineers.
Co. E 1st Gas Regiment.
2 Boundaries: Its zone of action and objective are those of the division.

(b) Division Reserve:
159th Brigade.
314th Machine Gun Bn.
1 company 305th Engineers
3. At H plus 3 hours the line (also 77th Division) advances from the First Objective.

3-3

4. At H plus 6 hours and 30 minutes the line advances from the Second Objective.

(a) The 313th and 314th Machine Gun Battalions will, under direction of the Division Machine Gun Officer, execute long range overhead and indirect fire from H minus 1 hour to the time limit of safety of the infantry advance. After the execution of this fire these battalions will not move forward but will revert to the Division Reserve.

(b) Combat troops will be in position at D day at H minus 4 hours. The attack will be pushed with the utmost vigor.

IV. LIAISON:

(a) The Commanding General, 160th Brigade, will provide a combat liaison detachment of one company of infantry and one machine gun platoon to connect with a similar detachment of the left division of the 5th Corps (2nd Division). The command of this combined detachment will be designated by the Commanding Brig. Gen. of the 2d Division.

(b) Details of combat liaison with the 77th Division on the left will be indicated later.

(c) Axis of Liaison: - CHEHERY - FLEVILLE - ST. JUVIN - ALLIEPONT - SIVRY lez BUZANCY - BUZANCY - FOSSE.

V. COMMAND POSTS:
80th Division: CHEHERY
2d Division: CHARPENTRY
77th Division: CHEHERY
160th Brigade: SOMMERANCE
159th Brigade: POINT 04.08
Div. Artillery: CHEHERY

A. CRONKHITE

Major General, Commanding.

The reader will note that for this particular operation ("FIELD ORDER NO. 27"), "the 313th and 314th M.G. Battalions will, under direction of the division machine gun officer, execute long range overhead and indirect fire from H minus 1 hour to the time limit of safety of the infantry advance. After the execution of this fire these battalions will not move forward but will revert to the division reserve." By this time in the war, we had become convinced of the utility of M.G. barrages and accepted the fact that M.G.s took lots of time and effort to get to the front line of troops. In the mean time, why not shoot out several belts of 30.06 in a barrage!? On Oct. 30, P.F.C. Howard L. Ashcroft of D/2/314th Artillery was cited for bravery while serving at an O.P. with an infantry outfit of the 5th (Red Diamond) Division: "On the night of Oct. 30, 1918, near Romagne, P.F.C. Ashcroft, being stationed at the battalion O.P. as telephone operator, repaired several breaks in the line during the night under heavy enemy shell fire."[140]

October 31, 1918.

Weather: Fair.

Roads: Good.

On Oct. 31, 1918 (Halloween), the 80th Division, minus its artillery brigade, was attached to Maj. Gen. Joseph T. Dickman's American I Corps, which was advancing up the left of the Meuse-Argonne Sector. As such, America's Blue Ridge Division was ordered to move to a concentration area south of Cornay, a distance of some twenty-five km *via* the attack axes of the 77th (Metropolitan) and 28th (Red Keystone) Divisions during the first week of the great offensive.[141] Brett's 160th Inf. Brig. was to lead, followed by Cronkite's 159th Inf. Brig. Division assets were spread throughout. According to the Army, an infantry brigade took up about five km of road space. Dickman was an old cavalry officer from the Regular Army who had fought in the Apache Wars, the War with Spain, and in the Boxer Rebellion. Before this particular war, he was serving on the Army General Staff. In the A.E.F., Dickman had successfully commanded the 3rd (Rock of the Marne) Division at Chateau-Thierry and the IV Corps at Saint-Mihiel. Clearly, he was a "heavy."

---

[140] As cited in *314th Artillery*, 45.

[141] *Cornay* is pronounced "Cor-nay."

Thus ended the Battle of Bois d'Ogons for us in America's 80th (Blue Ridge) Division.

After the war, the Infantry regiments of the 80th Division were awarded four battle streamers. Of all of them, Phase II, or, for us, the battles for Bois d'Ogons and Ferme Madeleine, was the hardest one earned. In fighting through what we called "The Valley of Death," we suffered 3,551 casualties, including 1,154 Killed in Action (K.I.A.).

After Phase II, we were sent south to conduct Recovery Operations. There we received reinforcements and were issued not only brand new M1918 Browning Automatic Rifles (B.A.R.s), but also new M1917 Browning M.G.s. We were then sent to the left of the American First Army and fought up through the Sommerance, Immecourt, Sivry, Buzancy, Sommauthe, and Yoncq Corridor in Phase III. On Nov. 9, much to our chagrin, we were replaced by Pershing's "Fair-Haired Boys" of the 1st Infantry Division (If You're Going to be One, Be a Big Red One!) so it and Brig. Gen. Douglas MacArthur's 42nd (Rainbow) Divisions could seize Sedan, uncoupling the entire German line in France, Belgium, and Luxembourg. During this phase, we suffered 1,059 casualties, including 44 K.I.A.

In early summer 1919, what was left of us returned to the United States and exited the Army.

But we were not the same.

The 80th Division Only Moves Forward!

Bibliography.

"*313th Artillery*": Irving, Thomas and Edward Crowell. *A History of the 313th Artillery, U.S.A.* (New York: Thomas Y. Crowell Company, 1920).

"*314th Artillery*": *History of 314th Artillery* (314th Artillery Veterans' Association, N.D.).

"*314th M.G.*": *314th M.G. Battalion History, Blue Ridge (80th) Division. Published as a Matter of Record by the Officers and Men of the Battalion* (N.P., 1919).

"*317th Infantry*": Craighill, Edley, *History of the 317th Infantry Regiment, 80th Division* (N.P., N.D.).

"*318th Infantry*": *History of the 318th Infantry Regiment of the 80th Division, 1917-1919* (Richmond, Virginia: William Byrd Press, N.D.).

"*319th Infantry*": Peck, Josiah C. *The 319th Infantry A.E.F.* (Paris, France: Herbert Clarke Printing, 1919).

"*2/319th Infantry*": Herr, Charles Ryman. *Company F History, 319th Infantry* (N.P., 1920).

"*1/320th Infantry*": Williams, Ashby. *Experiences of the Great War: Artois, St. Mihiel, Meuse-Argonne* (Roanoke, Virginia: Press of the Stone Printing and Manufacturing Company, 1919).

"*3/320th Infantry*": Lukens, Edward C. *A Blue Ridge Memoir* (Baltimore, Maryland: Sun Print, 1922).

"*A.D.R.*": *Drill and Service Regulations for Field Artillery, 1917* (Washington, D.C., Government Printing Office, 1917).

"*A.B.M.C.*": *American Armies and Battlefields in Europe: A History, Guide, and Reference Book* (Washington, D.C.: Government Printing Office, American Battle Monuments Commission, 1938).

"*B.M.G.M.*": British General Staff. *Infantry Machine-Gun Company Training Manual, 1917.*

"Bullard": Bullard, Robert Lee, Maj. Gen. (U.S.A., ret). *Personalities and Reminiscences of the War* (Garden City, N.Y., 1925).

"*F.S.R.*": *Field Service Regulations, U.S. Army, 1914. Text Corrections to December 20, 1916.* (New York: Army and Navy Journal, 1916).

"Harbord": Harbord, James. *The American Army in France, 1917-19* (Boston: Little, Brown, and Company, 1936).

Hunt, Frazier: *Blown in by the Draft: Camp Yarns Collected at One of the Great National Army Cantonments by an Amateur War Correspondent. Forward by Col. Theodore Roosevelt.* (New York: Doubleday, Page, and Company, 1918).

"*I.D.R.*": *Infantry Drill Regulations, 1917.* (Washington, D.C.: Government Printing Office, 1917).

"*I.N.C.O.M.*": *Manual for Noncommissioned Officers and Privates of Infantry of the Army of the United States, 1917, to be used by Engineer companies (dismounted) and Coast Artillery companies for Infantry instruction and Training* (Government Printing Office, 1917).

"Mitchell": Mitchell, Lt. Col. William A. *Outlines of Military History* (Washington, D.C.: National Service Publishing Company, 1931).

"*M.G.D.R.*": *Drill Regulations for Machine Guns: Infantry, 1917* (Washington, D.C., Government Printing Office, 1917).

"*M.M.T.*": Moss, Col. James. *Manual of Military Training* (Menasha, Wisconsin: Army and College Printers, 1917).

"*M.S.T.*": *Drill and Service Manual for Sanitary Troops, U.S.A., April 15, 1917.*

"*N.C.O.M.A.*": *Manual for N.C.O.s and Privates of Field Artillery of the A.U.S., 1917* (Washington, D.C., Government Printing Office, 1917).

"Pershing": Pershing, John Joseph. *My Experiences in the World War* (New York: F.A. Stokes, 1931), 2 volumes.

"*P.M.*": Ellis, O.O. and E.B. Garey, Majors, U.S. Army Infantry. *Plattsburg Manual*: *A Handbook for Military Training* (New York, The Century Company, 1917).

"Stultz": Stultz, Sgt. Russell Lee. *History of the 80th Division, A.E.F.* (80th Division Veterans' Association, 1923).

"*T.O.E., 1914*": *Tables of Organization Based on the Field Service Regulations of 1914* (Washington, D.C., War Department, 1914).

Young, Rush, S. *Over the Top with the 80th, by a Buck Private* (N.P., 1933).

About the Author

Author, historian, and Army Major Gary Schreckengost (ret.) is a life member of the 80th Division Association (80thdivision.com). A Cold War, Homeland, Bosnia, and Iraq War veteran, Schreckengost is the author of *The 80th Division in Iraq: Iraqi Army Advisors in Action, Achtung Panzer, Marsch! With the 1st German Panzer Division: Formation to the Fall of France, 1935-40,* and *Wheat's Tigers: The 1st Louisiana Special Battalion in the Civil War.* His other works have been published in *America's Civil War Magazine, World War II Magazine, Field Artillery Journal,* and *Armor Magazine.*

The four books in this series, found on Amazon.com, are:

The 80th Division in World War I, Volume 1: Camp Lee to Saint-Mihiel.

The 80th Division in World War I, Volume 2: Meuse-Argonne to Homecoming.

The 80th Division in World War I: Into the Meuse-Argonne, Sept.-Nov. 1918.

The 80th Division in World War I: The Battle for Bois d'Ogons, Oct. 4-6, 1918.

Other 80th Division Books on Amazon.com

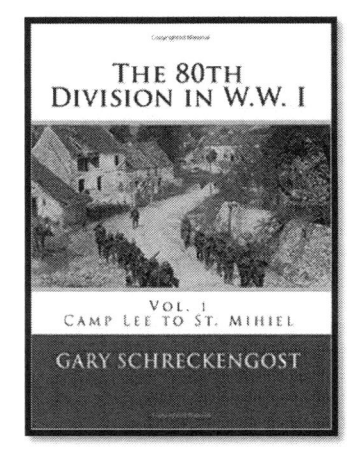

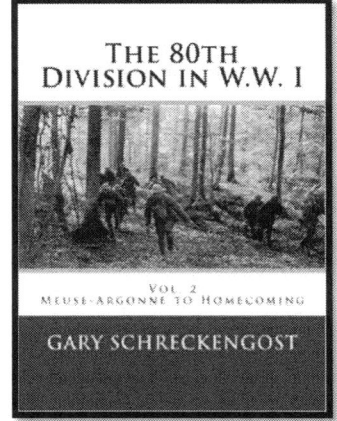

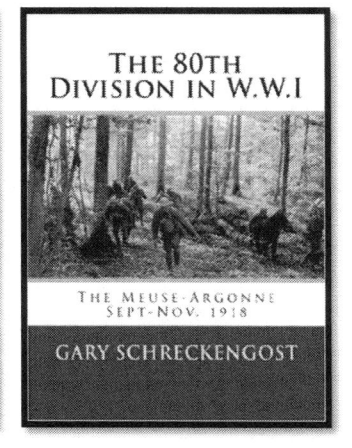

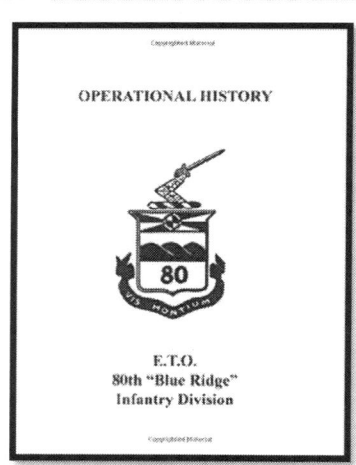

Made in the USA
Middletown, DE
08 October 2018